Growing A Great Marriage

Bob & Emilie Barnes

HARVEST HOUSE PUBLISHERS
Eugene, Oregon 97402

GROWING A GREAT MARRIAGE

Copyright © 1988 by Harvest House Publishers
Eugene, Oregon 97402

Library of Congress Cataloging-in-Publication Data

Barnes, Bob.
  Growing a great marriage.

    1. Marriage—Religious aspects—Christianity
2. Barnes, Bob.   3. Barnes, Emilie.   I. Barnes, Emilie.
II. Title.
BV835.B344 1988   248.4   87-83694
ISBN 0-89081-677-8

This book would not have been possible except for some wonderful Christians who have taken time to contribute to our lives. Over the years there have been pastors, teachers, friends, neighbors, seminars, retreats, tapes, and books which have helped us formulate our marriage life-style. We give all the credit for our marriage to the tremendous Christian support we have received over the years.

The number one influence in our marriage has been the Bible. Without reading, studying, and applying its principles for life and marriage, Emilie and I could very well have ended up a tragic marriage statistic.

We dedicate this book especially to our two children, Jenny and Brad. They were a joy as children and continue to be blessings as adults. Their cooperation has been greatly appreciated.

We want to encourage each of you who read this book to dedicate your life to showing the world what Christ and the Church are all about through your marriage. Our theme verse for growing a great marriage has been Ephesians 5:21: "Submit to one another out of reverence for Christ" (NIV). Only when we first humble ourselves before the Lord are we able to submit ourselves to one another. Keep pride off the throne of your life and let Jesus Christ be your power source.

Dedicate yourself to your mate. May Jesus Christ always be glorified in our marriages.

Contents

INTRODUCTION

Welcome to Our Marriage Garden

Growing a Great Marriage is a love story about two ordinary young people who fell in love, were married, and have enjoyed more than 33 years together. It's about how we grew a great marriage, and how you can grow a great marriage too. Our book is not a manual full of foolproof theories, magic steps, or super formulas. Rather, we approach our view of marriage with a life-style flavor. Emilie and I want to share with you how we learned to be faithful to God's Word in our marriage, and how He has been faithful to bless our life together. Ours is not the story of two perfect people, but two growing people who decided to be obedient to God's Word and to employ His principles.

My family background is in farming, so it seemed natural for us to talk about marriage as something which needs to be nurtured and cultivated like a garden. A good marriage, like a good crop, doesn't come easy. A couple needs to work at growing a great relationship. You must understand the seasons, cooperate with God's laws for growing things, and watch out for weeds. And just as good crops need the sun, great marriages need the Son. Our story centers on the Lord Jesus Christ, the Son of God and the anchor of our life together. Without Him there would be no great marriage for us, and no great marriage book.

We use the word *great* to describe our marriage in all humility. Only by being obedient to God and His Word can we call our marriage great. According to Romans 8:16-17, Emilie and I are God's children and joint heirs with Christ. In spite of all our differences, Emilie and I have a great marriage because we are both related to Christ and submitted to Him in each other. Wherever we travel we meet couples who are enjoying great marriages. In each case we find two people who are willing to submit to God, submit to each other, and obey God's Word.

We have written these chapters from the foundation of Scripture and from the perspective of our life experience. As you will notice, Emilie wrote several of the chapters and I wrote the rest. But every chapter reflects our combined thoughts on each subject. We have included practical examples from our marriage and the lives of many others we know. Furthermore, the content of this book has been influenced by more than 33 years of reading, listening, and talking, and by countless stories, illustrations, and quotes on marriage we have collected. We have attempted to give proper credit to our sources. In some cases we don't remember the original source, but we felt the material was valuable to illustrate a point.

Our hearts ache from seeing the hurts and agony in marriages today resulting from selfish mates who want their own way and who are unwilling to submit to one another. Marriage relationships are floundering, wracked by doubt, distrust, infidelity, and disregard for the marriage vows. Our society has a false impression of what true marriage is because of the distorted view presented on television, in the movies, and in today's literature. Couples keep *receiving* the wrong message about marriage because our society keeps *sending* the wrong message about marriage.

In the face of a persistent, negative tide, Christian couples today must learn to tend their gardens and grow great marriages. They need to work through the problems which spring up in their relationships. They need to cultivate patience, good communication, trust, and commitment. They need to activate their marriage vows and adopt the spiritual dimension in order to see their marriages through.

We trust that the resources and information in this book will help you in your gardening. We want to serve as a positive model which encourages you and equips you to roll up your sleeves and grow a great marriage.

1

Great Marriages Aren't Made They're Grown

> For this cause a man shall leave his father
> and his mother, and shall cleave to his wife;
> and they shall become one flesh. And the
> man and his wife were both naked and were
> not ashamed (Gen. 2:24,25, NASB).

When I was about 20 years old, over a year before I met Emilie, God gave me a burning desire to move out of my home and find a residence of my own. At the same time He gave me a desire to marry and raise a family. I knew God was preparing me to share my life with a very special woman. At that point, however, I had no idea who that woman would be.

As part of my preparation, God led me to Genesis 2:24,25. As I studied these verses, four areas of emphasis stood out to me:

DEPARTURE: A man shall leave his
father and mother...

PERMANENCE: And shall cleave to his
wife...

ONENESS: And they shall become one
flesh...

SEXUALITY: And the man and his wife
were both naked and were not ashamed.

Emilie and I can recommend from our experience that these four areas constitute four critical stepping-stones for growing a great marriage. Let's talk about them in greater detail.

Departure

Departure means to sever the ties of emotional attachment, financial assistance, and the security and general protection we receive from our parents. Departure from our original families was not very difficult for Emilie or me. Emilie's father died during her childhood, so there was no tie to break with him. Her brother had been a problem for several years, so it was not difficult to sever that trying relationship. And since she was to remain geographically close to her mother after our marriage, Emilie's separation from her did not prove to be a hardship.

Midway through college I moved out of my parents' home to become a live-in caretaker for the estate of a very wealthy family. My parents had raised all three of their sons to be weaned from the home as young men. As such, departure from my parents to marry Emilie was not a problem for me.

According to Genesis 2:24, men are instructed to leave their parents in preparation for marriage. The first step is for us men (and women as well) to leave physically by moving out of the home to be on our own. In some cases a departing man or woman may need to secure an apartment with a roommate to share living expenses. We also need to make an important emotional break. Many adults are still controlled by their parents because they have never consciously stepped away from their parents' control. The emotional separation doesn't mean we no longer care for our parents. It means we are no longer under their parental control.

Financial independence is a very important aspect of leaving the parental home. Leaving financially means we are free to accept financial assistance from our parents, but we no longer depend on them for it. Emilie and I know several adults who are financially irresponsible because they are waiting for an inheritance from their parents. They have never taken responsibility for their own finances because they are hoping Dad and Mom's money will someday bail them out.

As parents we need to assist our adult children in making this transition as smoothly as possible. Unfortunately a child's departure is often the end result of many harsh words or hurtful actions. Hopefully the transition is a natural part of the family cycle; something the parents and the child have prepared for.

We heard the following departure letter read by a mother on Dr. James Dobson's radio program, "Focus on the Family":

Dear Paul:

This is the most important letter I have ever written to you, and I hope you will take it as seriously as it is intended. I have given a great amount of thought and prayer to the matter I want to convey, and believe I am right in what I've decided to do.

For the past several years, you and I have been involved in a painful tug-of-war. You have been struggling to free yourself of my values and my wishes for your life. At the same time, I have been trying to hold you to what we both know is right. Even at the risk of nagging, I have been saying, "Go to church," "Choose the right friends," "Make good grades in school," "Live a Christian life," "Prepare wisely for your future," etc. I'm sure you've gotten tired of this urging and warning, but I have only wanted the best for you. This is the only way I knew to keep you from making some of the mistakes so many others have made.

However, I've thought all of this over during the last month and I believe that my job as your mother is now finished. Since the day you were born, I have done my best to do what was right for you. I have not always been successful—I've made mistakes and I've failed in many ways. Someday you will learn how difficult it is to be a good parent, and perhaps then you'll understand me better than you do now. But there's one area where I have never wavered: I've loved you with everything that is within me. It is impossible to convey the depth of my love for you through these years, and that affection is as great today as it's ever been. I will continue to be there in the future, although our relationship will change from this moment. As of now, you are free! You may reject God or accept Him, as you choose. Ultimately, you will answer only to Him, anyway. You may marry whomever you wish without protest from me. You may go to U.C.L.A. or U.S.C. or any other college of your selection. You may fail or succeed in each of life's responsibilities. The umbilical cord is broken.

I am not saying these things out of bitterness or anger. I still care what happens to you and am concerned for your welfare. I will pray for you daily, and if you come to me for advice, I'll offer my opinion. *But the responsibility now shifts from my shoulders to yours.* You are a man now, and you're entitled to make your own decisions— regardless of the consequences. Throughout your life I've tried to build a foundation of values which would prepare you for this moment of manhood and independence. That time has come, and my record is in the books.

I have confidence in you, son. You are gifted and have been blessed in so many ways. I believe God will lead you and guide your footsteps, and I am optimistic about the future. Regardless of the outcome, I will always have a special tenderness in my heart for my beloved son.

Dad

Each family is rather unique in how it releases its children into adulthood and marriage. In the Jewish wedding ceremonies we have attended, parents of the bride and groom recite vows releasing their children from parental authority. This might be a good tradition to add to our Christian ceremony. Formally releasing our children can serve to eliminate a lot of guilt—in us and our kids—which often attends a child's departure to marry.

We often cling to our children because we fear they are exiting our lives completely. But departure doesn't mean that we will no longer see them, have them over for dinner, or counsel them when they seek it. But it does mean that we no longer try to control them as we did when they were younger.

Permanence

The Hebrew word translated "cleave" means to cling or to be glued. God intends husband and wife to be bonded to one another permanently. Marriage is not a trial run; it's a once-and-for-all union.

In Deuteronomy 24:5, God gave husbands and wives a formula for entering into the permanence which He intended for cleaving couples: "When a man takes a new wife, he shall not go out with the army, nor be charged with any duty; he shall be free at home one year and shall give happiness to his wife whom he has taken" (NASB). The Israeli bridegroom was commanded to set all his other responsibilities aside for one year in order to concentrate on giving happiness to his wife. It was a period of time for a couple to get to know one another and establish permanence.

Few newlyweds today have the resources to quit their jobs in order to spend every moment of their first year alone together. But there are some practical steps all married couples can take to apply or reinforce the glue of permanence in their marriages.

First, leave your parents' home and set up a home of your own. If at all possible, do not live in the same house with either of your parents, even if it is more economical to do so.

Second, spend as much time as possible together. Get your priorities straight about your nights out with the boys or girls. Many marriages get off to a rocky start because the husband wants to keep his busy schedule of hunting, fishing, or bowling with the boys and the wife continues spending her spare time with her girlfriends. Our spouses are more important than our friends. We can't build permanence if we don't spend time together—especially when first married. Your old friends may have difficulty adjusting to your time commitment to your spouse. But they will understand if you explain your new responsibilities.

Third, keep the television out of your bedroom. The bedroom should be reserved for sleeping and loving. Many wives complain that their husbands come to bed to finish a movie or a ball game, or to watch the late news. The television robs many couples of the happiness they should be providing each other in the bedroom.

Oneness

God says that a husband and wife "shall become one flesh." In God's sight we become one at the altar with our vows of commitment. But practically speaking, oneness between a husband and wife is a process that happens over a period of time—your lifetime together.

It is very difficult to move from only caring for yourself to sharing your entire life with another person. And the older you are when you marry, the more difficult it becomes because you are more set in your ways. Emilie and I had very different backgrounds in family, religion, finances, tastes, and holiday celebrations. She came from the home of a verbally and physically abusive alcoholic father. I came from a warm, loving family where yelling and screaming were inappropriate. It took us only a few moments to enter into oneness by saying our vows. But we have spent more than 33 years blending our different lives and building the oneness which we enjoy today.

Oneness doesn't mean sameness. Oneness refers to an agreement in commitment, mission in life, goals, and dreams. We sometimes teach seminars in Oceanside, California, near the marine base at Camp Pendleton. It is easy to identify marines in Oceanside even when they aren't in uniform. There is an external conformity about them—short haircuts, muscular bodies, shiny shoes, straight backs, and a certain walk. But in marriage it is *internal* conformity, not *external* conformity, that expresses oneness.

The picture of oneness in marriage is that of total unselfishness as we allow God to shape each partner. Oneness emerges as two different individuals reflect the same Christ. And spiritual oneness produces tremendous strength and unity in a family.

One of Aesop's tales illustrates the strength of this inner unity. A farmer had a very quarrelsome family. After vainly trying to reconcile his bickering sons, the farmer decided to teach them by an example. He instructed his sons to bring him a bundle of sticks. After he tied the bundle securely, the farmer told his sons, one after the other, to break the bundle of sticks. They all tried and failed. Then the farmer untied the bundle and gave his sons the sticks to break one by one, which they did easily. The father said, "As long as you remain united you are a match for all your enemies. But separate and you are easily defeated."

To be one in marriage, a couple must be strong in the Lord. When we are one in Him, Satan cannot break us.

Sexuality

The Scriptures tell us that Adam and Eve "were both naked and were not ashamed." That was the age of innocence. But today we live in a society which is cluttered with the debris of fallen man. Every kind of marriage arrangement and nonmarriage relationship devised is exhibited in our culture. As I watch the television talk shows and hear the rich, the famous, the sex therapists, and the various movement leaders express their views on marriage, I pray that God will protect the hearers from all the garbage pouring out of these "experts." The only true expert on marriage is God, the one who designed it. And His manual on marriage is the Bible.

Before sin entered the world in the Garden of Eden, Adam and Eve lived naked and unashamed. The Hebrew word for "naked" simply means laid bare. Adam and Eve were completely open and transparent with each other; no hang-ups or embarrassments. Since they hid nothing from one another, they had nothing to be ashamed about.

It is no accident that this kind of openness in sexuality comes after departure, permanence, and oneness. When we give priority to the first three we will experience the fullness of sexuality as God designed it. Often we want sexuality to be first while we work on the other three, but that's not God's order. For example, we men have little difficulty becoming sexually stimulated and performing intercourse very quickly. But our wives are different and they don't respond quite as quickly. The setting must be just right, with no disturbances, and they need to be in a loving frame of mind. A wife will respond to sexual intimacy better if she knows that her man has made his break with his family and made her his top priority (departure), that he is totally committed to her (permanence), and that they share the same goals and dreams (oneness).

Many times sex in marriage is a frustrating struggle —a mixture of selfishness, embarrassment, dissatisfaction, and resentment. The key to a fulfilling sex life is openness and transparency between husband and wife. In a later chapter on communication we will deal more completely with the topic of transparency between two partners.

The Great Marriage

God's Word has been the foundation for a great marriage for Emilie and me. We have often said it in the form of an equation: **God's prescription plus our committed efforts equals marital fullness.** As we have worked to apply God's principles to our marriage we have discovered five principles for growing a great marriage. We use the following "great" acrostic to help us relate these principles to others:

G—Giving
R—Relating
E—Edifying
A—Allowing your mate to be God's person
T—Touching

Giving

The Scriptures speak often about two types of people: givers and takers. God's nature is to give and He is continually giving His free gifts to us. His plan is for us to be continual givers also. In our marriages that means we must give to one another our time, our talents, our hearts, ourselves, our love, our finances, our gifts, our thoughts, our trust, and our fears.

When Emilie and I stopped thinking about ourselves and started giving to each other, our relationship was strengthened. Some of the little gifts we have given each other which have received a positive response are: notes sent through the mail; a card of love tucked in a purse or lunch sack; words of encouragement; a bouquet of flowers; a new book which had been discussed; time in the evening for conversation; short mini-vacations together; and dinner out at least twice a month.

We found that when we started giving to each other it was easier for us to give to someone else. The circle of giving soon spread to people we didn't even know. The words of Charles H. Burr have been an inspiration to our giving: "Getters generally don't get happiness; givers get it. You simply give to others a bit of yourself—a thoughtful act, a helpful idea, a word of appreciation, a lift over a rough spot, a sense of understanding, a timely suggestion. You take something out of your mind, garnished in kindness out of your heart, and put it into the other fellow's mind and heart."

Relating

We live in a day when everyone wants to relate. The dictionary defines relating as one person connecting with another in thought and meaning. If any two people must connect in thought and meaning it is a husband and wife. Relating is a primary avenue to oneness in marriage.

Relating in marriage can only happen when partners spend much time together talking, listening, and learning what makes each other tick. This is very difficult for many who are unable to express themselves well. Emilie was very hesitant to speak during our early courtship because she feared she would say the wrong thing and blow our relationship. Since then she has made up for her shyness and now she has no trouble expressing herself to me.

A passage of Scripture we often use when teaching couples how to relate is Proverbs 24:3,4: "By wisdom a house is built, and by understanding it is established; and by knowledge the rooms are filled with all precious and pleasant riches" (NASB). Three key words stand out in these verses: *Wisdom, understanding*, and *knowledge*. We gain these three qualities by studying. In our marriages, we are to study our mates thoroughly in order to gain wisdom, understanding, and knowledge about them. How do we study them?

By relating to them through open, genuine conversation.

On Black Monday—October 19, 1987—the stock market took a sudden, severe nosedive, falling so fast that many sellers could not get out of the market in time to save their investments. Many investors lost thousands of dollars, some lost millions.

One man I heard about lost $250,000 on Black Monday. How would you react if you watched a quarter of a million dollars disappear before your very eyes? Would you jump off a bridge or go get drunk? Fortunately, this man had learned that his home was a "trauma center." He phoned his wife and calmly told her what had happened. Then he asked her for a date that evening. They went out to dinner and discussed the day's happenings together, just like they had done many times before over far less shattering events. Thank the Lord this couple had learned to relate.

Relating doesn't happen automatically. As my grandfather taught me as we sat behind the wheel of his John Deere tractor, growing things takes a lot of hard, well-planned work. Marital wisdom, understanding, and knowledge only grow strong through many patient hours of relating. But there is a reward for our labors. The "precious and pleasant riches" we gain from our efforts are positive attitudes, good relationships, pleasant memories, mutual respect, and depth of character.

Edifying

Our verse for this concept is Ephesians 4:29: "Let no corrupt communication proceed out of your mouth, but that which is good to the use of edifying, that it may minister grace unto the hearers" (KJV). As the verse suggests, communication is a major channel by which we edify one another. In our chapter on communication we will spend more time discussing ways to succeed in good communication.

When we edify our mates we lift them up. Whenever Emilie or I find ourselves talking about other people negatively, we remind ourselves to be positive by asking each other, "Is this edifying?" As soon as that question is voiced our conversation becomes more positive. Each husband and wife would do well to keep that question in the forefront of his or her mind to make sure the conversation between them is edifying.

We have found these lines by Ida Goldsmith Morris helpful in keeping our conversation positive:

> It takes so little to make us sad,
> Just a slighting word or doubting sneer,
> Just a scornful smile on some lips held dear;
> And our footsteps lag, though the goal
>   seemed near,
> And we lose our courage and hope we had—
> So little it takes to make us sad.
>
> It takes so little to make us glad,
> Just a cheering clasp of a friendly hand,
> Just a word from one who can understand;
> And we finish the task we long had planned,
> And we lose the doubt and the fear we had—
> So little it takes to make us glad.

Allowing Your Mate to Be God's Person

One of the hardest lessons about trusting God in our marriages is allowing God to be the change agent in your mate. Far too often we think we are ordained by God to change our husband or wife (and later, the children).

One way to deal with the urge to change our mates is to concentrate on the positives and let God deal with the negatives. You might use a chart like the one below to help you identify your mate's strengths and formulate how you will cooperate with God in securing desired changes.

Category of Expectation	Strengths	Desired Changes	Action for Change
1. Personal habits	very neat picks up clothes hangs towels puts away shoes	to take a shower each day to shampoo hair regularly to use under-arm cologne	to talk to him about these areas to buy him his own shampoo, cologne let God work in this area
2. Children	_____	_____	_____
3. Finances	_____	_____	_____
4. Sex	_____	_____	_____
5. Spiritual	_____	_____	_____
6. Social	_____	_____	_____
7. Aspirations	_____	_____	_____
8. Time	_____	_____	_____

Emilie and I have always wanted the best for each other. One of our goals has been to avoid competition with each other. If one of us gets lifted up in some way, the other says, "Thank you, God, for blessing Bob/Emilie."

For the many years I was in education and business, Emilie was always known as Bob's wife. But for the last several years, since God has blessed Emilie's speaking and writing ministry, I have been known as Emilie's husband. (Occasionally I am introduced as Mr. Emilie Barnes!) Quite frankly, this reversal initially was a threat to me, even though I was excited to see God use Emilie and her gifts in ministry. I had always been the provider and I enjoyed being in the spotlight. Then suddenly I was playing second fiddle to my wife. God dealt with me for several years in this area. I had to continually ask myself if I wanted to glorify Bob or Jesus Christ. Every time the answer was Jesus, but it took me a while to anchor this concept in my heart. Now I can honestly say that as long as Jesus is lifted up in our ministries, I will serve in whatever capacity He wants to use me.

It's so easy to get caught up in the world's mind-set of being in competition with your mate. Satan would love to divide your strengths, talents, and gifts by seeing you work against each other. He will prey on your insecurities to drive a wedge between you and fracture your unity.

Become encouragers to one another instead. Be excited about your mate's successes. And comfort your partner when the contract isn't signed, the deal falls through, sickness slows you down, your license isn't renewed, children stray from the faith, etc. If we learn to submit to each other by the power of the Holy Spirit, we can allow each other to be God's person.

Touching

Can you remember when a parent, teacher, or coach wrapped his arm around you or patted you gently to indicate that everything was going to be okay? A loving touch seems to have healing power and communicates that we are accepted. If children live with touching parents they will learn to trust people and will be touchers themselves in adult life. We had a saying around our home that everybody needed at least four hugs a day to stay healthy.

Touching is also an important element in a great marriage. Emilie and I have found touching to be an excellent way by which partners can transmit helpful encouragement to each other. Unfortunately, when choosing a mate we seldom consider if the prospective partner is a toucher. Some of us came from very affectionate families, some did not. It is difficult for non-touchers to become touchers, but with prayer and patience even the most reserved non-toucher can become a loving toucher.

In our seminars and counseling we meet many women who wish their husbands would express their affection by simply holding their hands, hugging them, or cozying up with them on the couch. Men seem to want to get to the bedroom as soon as possible. But most women want the tenderness of touching—and it doesn't always need to lead to the bedroom.

Affectionate touching between Mom and Dad also serves as a signal to the children that their parents love each other. Kids are comforted by the security of knowing that their parents are lovingly committed to each other.

These five elements of a great marriage don't just happen. They must be cultivated and nourished just like a good crop. And the mere presence of these elements doesn't guarantee the success of the marriage. But they certainly hold the potential to enrich an already strong marriage or energize a slumping marriage.

The following lines are worth reading, rereading, and pondering. They communicate volumes about a great marriage:

- ❧ All marriages aren't happy; living together is tough.

- ❧ A good marriage is not a gift; it's an achievement by God's grace.

- ❧ Marriage is not for children; it takes guts and maturity.

- ❧ Marriage separates the men from the boys and the women from the girls.

- ❧ Marriage is tested daily by the ability to compromise.

- ❧ The survival of marriage can depend on being smart enough to know what's worth fighting about, making an issue of, or even mentioning.

- ❧ Marriage is giving, and more importantly, forgiving.

- ❧ With all its ups and downs, marriage is still God's best object lesson of Jesus and the Church.

- ❧ Through submission to one another we can witness to the world that marriage does work and is still alive.

- ❧ Marriage is worth dying for. If we give it proper honor, we will be honored by our children, our families, our neighbors, our friends, and—best of all—our Lord.

2

The Growing of a Wife-to-Be

> For we know that in all things God works
> for good with those who love him, those
> whom he has called according to his purpose
> (Rom. 8:28, TEV).

Irene was a Jewish girl born in Brooklyn, New York, the oldest of five children. Her mother died during the birth of Irene's baby sister. And Papa, a gifted tailor, died a few years later, leaving teenaged Irene to raise her brothers and sisters. Jobs and money were in California, so the young family headed for Hollywood to make a life for themselves.

As a young adult, Irene designed and sewed tennis dresses for movie stars in the early 1920s. She worked hard to support herself and her brothers and sisters. At 29 she met Otto Klein, a 40-year-old chef for Paramount Studios. Irene married Otto in 1930.

Irene badly wanted children but Otto wouldn't hear of it. As a German Jew and a veteran of World War I, Otto had barely escaped the war with his life. He wasn't about to bring children into such an angry world. Twice Irene became pregnant and twice he forced her into abortions. When she became pregnant a third time, Irene refused to terminate the pregnancy. In July 1934, a beautiful son, Edmund Francis

Klein, was born to Otto and Irene. Four years later, on April 12, 1938, Emilie Marie Klein was born. Otto adored his baby daughter, but his young son Edmund became the abused victim of a father filled with hatred from abuse he suffered as a child.

Otto was a creative and artistic man. As an orphan in Vienna he was placed in the palace to be a kitchen helper. His exceptional ability gained him training by the finest chefs in Europe and Otto became an expert Viennese chef. He escaped war-torn Europe, traveling first to New York and then to Hollywood. There he became a chef to movie stars—Clark Gable, Mickey Rooney, Lana Turner, Greta Garbo, Mario Lanza, Douglas Fairbanks, Judy Garland, and many more. Yet deep inside this successful man was a little boy still hurting from the loss of his parents.

Otto turned to alcohol to escape his pain, jeopardizing his career and his family. Otto's drinking fueled his angry perfectionism, resulting in violent outbursts at the shortcomings of his co-workers, wife, and children.

Irene's fear for the safety of herself and her children smothered her fun-loving, sanguine temperament. Edmund stored his anger for his abusive father, releasing it later in rebellion. And Emilie—that's me—became a very bashful, quiet child.

I have only a few happy memories of my father. When I was nine years old we moved to Long Beach, California, where Daddy managed a restaurant called Ormando's. He would take me on walks along the beach and we would fish off the pier. He gave me a beautiful blue bicycle on my tenth birthday.

Daddy lost his job at Ormando's due to his temper and drinking problem. My brother Edmund, who was almost 14 at the time, began his years of rebellion. Then Daddy became very ill. He refused to listen to his doctors. Instead he got mad at them and demanded that they make him well.

Because of my father, the emotional thermometer in our home was almost always on high. It was my job to try to keep peace and I was able to cool Daddy's temper at times. He adored me and never abused me. But I hurt inside because of what he did to my mother and brother. I suffered from nightmares, and I wished Daddy would die and relieve us of the control he held over us with his hot temper.

Daddy didn't let Mama cook very often because she didn't meet his gourmet standards. But she was also a great cook. Her corned beef cabbage rolls and other Jewish meals are a delicious memory. Occasionally Mama and Daddy would prepare a meal together, and I would sit on the drain board watching and learning. Those were happy days for me—probably because Daddy wasn't drinking on those days.

The summer after my eleventh birthday my wish came true. Daddy died and we were released from his bondage. I cried as I looked toward heaven wondering about the afterlife. But I quickly pushed those thoughts out of my mind. Mama was now a single mother with two children to care for. Being unemployed and uninsured, Daddy left us with hospital and doctor bills.

My aunt and uncle kept us afloat financially and helped my mother open up a small dress shop in Long Beach. We lived in a three-room apartment behind the store—kitchen, living room, and one bedroom. It was perfect for our needs. We gave Edmund the bedroom and Mama and I slept together in a Murphy bed in the living room. Mama gave me the responsibility of caring for those three rooms while she ran the dress shop. I painted the whole apartment myself, even though I had never painted in my life. I decorated the walls and, with help from Mama, made curtains, tablecloths, and chair covers. I planted flowers in our window box and kept the bathroom and kitchen spotless. Under Mama's direction I prepared the meals and washed the laundry.

Mama was a Proverbs 31 woman and didn't even know it. She was a hard worker, often working at the shop late into the night. She watched for bargains in order to make our money go farther. Together we transformed our simple apartment into a haven of peace.

My brother shattered our peaceful home, making it a home filled with stress and worry. His teachers called, the principal called, and then Edmund was kicked out of school. Several times the police called Mama in the early morning hours, telling her that Edmund was in jail. Mama and I would get up, wait for the city bus, and travel to the police station to identify him. Poor Mama was heartbroken over her son. Finally Edmund enlisted in the Marines, and a few years later he was married.

Mama was able to work us out of debt, so we moved to a larger apartment away from the store. By this time I was in complete control of our apartment— washing, ironing, planning meals. I was also going to school, working in our dress shop, and traveling with Mama to the garment district in Los Angeles once a month to buy dresses. My mother had trained me well.

During the years following Daddy's death, we became active in our local Jewish temple. On Wednesdays after public school I attended Hebrew school taught by the rabbi. At 15 I was confirmed at the temple and my family was proud of their little Jewish girl. But my confirmation didn't bring peace to my heart, and I still didn't have the answer to my questions about life after death.

At age 16 I attended a modeling class at the Wilma Hastings Modeling School. It was there that I met Esther, the most talented, beautiful, and natural model in our class. Esther later went to New York and became a high fashion model, appearing on the cover of several fashion magazines.

Esther stayed with me a week that summer. We went to the beach, worked in our dress shop, and played "fashion show." One evening we went to the movies and there met Bill Barnes. Bill wanted to date Esther, but Esther and I had made an agreement that we would only double date. Esther told Bill that he would have to find a date for her girlfriend Emilie. Bill's identical twin Bob owed him a favor, so Bob Barnes became my blind date.

I was immediately attracted to Bob by his deep tan, faded denim pants, white shirt, and saddle shoes. He was a mature college student, athletic and strong. He opened the doors for me, displayed gracious manners, and carried himself with an air of gentleness. There was something very different about him.

Esther and I had been experimenting with cigarettes and planned to smoke in front of these college men to show them how mature we were. When Esther offered me a cigarette I heard a voice inside me say, "Don't do it!" So I refused, and was I ever glad. Later we discovered that Bill and Bob didn't smoke, and I wanted Bob to be impressed with me.

I was shy, bashful, and very quiet during our blind date. I figured that if I didn't talk a lot I wouldn't say the wrong thing and reveal my age. I didn't want to blow it with Bob Barnes.

I was absolutely shocked when Bob called me for a real date. On the day of our date I cleaned the house, baked cookies, washed and set my hair, polished my nails, and washed and ironed clothes. I prepared the atmosphere by lighting candles and boiling cinnamon sticks on the stove to give the apartment a homey aroma. I wanted everything to be perfect—even the things he wouldn't see when he came to pick me up.

Being the homemaker of the century, I won the heart of my man—except for one area. I was a Jewish girl and Bob was a committed Christian. Mama really liked Bob, a clean-cut gentleman. But my aunts and uncles were outraged that Mama allowed me to date a Gentile, worse yet, a "dyed-in-the-wool Baptist" as they called him. "You are making a big mistake, Irene," they told Mama. "He'll never amount to anything. He's not good enough for our Emilie. They'll have a miserable life. She's too young, so send him away. Better yet, send her away."

Even though I didn't know it at the time, God was in control. By the time I was 16 our relationship was growing deep and serious. Bob's family was praying for me during those dating months as Bob patiently read the Scriptures to me, took me to church, directed me to messages by Billy Graham, and introduced me to his Christian friends. One verse that pierced my heart was John 14:6: "Jesus answered, 'I am the way and the truth and the life. No one comes to the Father except through me' " (NIV). I asked myself, *Is Jesus the Messiah our people are waiting for?*

Then I read Romans 6:23: "The wages of sin is death, but the gift of God is eternal life in Christ Jesus our Lord" (NIV). *Eternal life—is that the answer to an 11-year-old's questions about life after death? Can I have life forever and ever by believing in Jesus Christ and receiving Him into my heart? Is dying merely a change of address from earth to heaven?*

Bob gently guided me into the family of God. One night, in the quietness of my room, I knelt, opened the door of my heart, and invited the Lord Jesus—

Messiah Yeshua—into my life. I asked Him to change me and give me a heart ready to serve Him. I asked Him to take control of me and guide me on a path that would please Him.

Having cleared the only hurdle between us, I wanted to marry Bob Barnes and build a healthy, happy, spiritual home free from abuse and anger; a home with harmony, love, and the fragrance of Jesus. I knew we could have that kind of home, even though the path would be rocky at times. But Bob and I were committed to the common goal of serving the Lord and serving each other. We could survive with God's help.

The criticism from my family grew strong, especially after we announced our engagement. My aunt and uncle offered to send me to one of the best finishing schools in Europe, buy me a car and a wardrobe, and provide me an unlimited expense account if I would not marry Bob. But my heart now belonged to God and to Bob. I had already received the greatest gift—God's Son, Messiah Jesus—with no strings attached. I told my aunt and uncle that I loved them, but I was going to marry Bob and establish a Christian home.

In September 1955, Bob—age 22—and I—age 17— were married. Yes, my relatives' hearts were broken. Family pressure was heavy on Mama who agreed to sign for me to marry at my young age. But, thank God, I was not disowned or "buried" as some Jews are when they marry outside the faith. My family didn't think our marriage would last more than a few months. But we had a loving God guiding our hearts and lives.

Shortly after our wedding I began my senior year of high school and Bob began his first year of teaching. I wasn't much older than his students. Bob helped me with term papers, signed my report cards, and attended senior activities with me. I received the homemaker of the year award, starred in the senior play, and served as student body secretary as the only married student at Long Beach Poly High School.

After graduation I kept house, worked in the dress shop, and later took a job with a bank. I wanted a family, but Bob felt we should wait until we could afford a house and he was secure in his school district. Three years later our daughter Jennifer Christine was born.

Just a few months after Jennifer arrived we became parents to three more children. My brother Edmund's wife left for the market one day and never returned home, walking out on her husband and three preschool children—Tawney, Keri, and Kevin. We have seen her only once in over 30 years, and she has never contacted her children. Edmund became very depressed and was unable to care for his children. Bob and I felt the children needed love and stability, so we asked Edmund if he would let us take them into our home. We soon became legal guardians for Tawney, Keri, and Kevin.

Mothering four children under the age of four was an exhausting job. I cooked, baked, cleaned, washed, ironed, and did everything I could to create a loving home for our family. I made all the children's clothes, plus my own. Whenever Bob wasn't refereeing football or basketball games he was home by 4:00 P.M., which was a great help to me. I was happy that my childhood responsibilities had equipped me with the tools I needed—another proof that God works all things together for His purposes.

A few weeks after Edmund's children came, I discovered that I was pregnant. I was so sick with number five that it was difficult to carry on with the other four.

One day I was so sick that I took the four kids into the backyard, spread a blanket on the grass, and passed out. I didn't care if they ate dirt or snails while I slept; I wouldn't need to feed them lunch.

Another day three-year-old Keri got into some paint cans in our neighbor's garage. I found her covered head to toe in red oil-based paint. After stripping her clothes and cleaning her with paint remover and a warm bath, I put us both down for a nap. Fifteen minutes later she was back into the paint again.

In May 1960, our son Bradley Joe Barnes was born, giving us five children under five years of age—and I was only 21. My mother was still running the dress shop so she was unable to help me. Bob was a great help, but he had a profession, night classes, and a part-time refereeing job. So raising the children was my baby in more ways than one. I survived the next few years until Edmund remarried. His wife had two children, so when Edmund's three went back to him they had a family of seven.

By this time Mama's business had faltered and she filed for bankruptcy. She lost what little she had and slipped into a deep depression. She was in her early 60s with no home, no job, and no future. We invited Mama to live with us until she could reorganize her life. Mama's visit turned out to be another step in the path of God's plan. Being in our home, she attended church with us and the Spirit of God touched her heart. In 1964 Mama invited the Messiah into her life. At this writing she is the only one of my family members to come into the Christian family. But I'm not giving up on my family. John 14:14 says: "If you ask me for anything in my name, I will do it" (TEV). I'm trusting our Lord for each of my family members, and He will answer.

Bob and I continued to raise our family, and as I grew up with the children we learned much together. Bob and I were committed to God, family, love, goals, and raising responsible adults. I worked at being industrious, creative, and very organized in our family life, which gave me more hours in my day—the title of my first book.

At age 29 I became the first chairwoman of the Newport Beach Christian Women's Club. That year I was asked to speak to over 800 women at a conference in Palm Springs. I was so naive and absolutely scared to death. But the response to my testimony overwhelmed me. Other chairwomen asked me to speak at their meetings. Rose Tiffany, a long-time Christian friend who supported me in prayer that day, answered, "She'll come," and started booking dates. Since that time I have spoken to several hundred Christian Women's Clubs.

In 1971 we moved from Newport Beach to Riverside, California. I was 33 years old. Our years in Newport Beach had gained us some very close friends and church relationships. We had grown spiritually so much at Mariners Church that it was hard to begin again. By this time Mama had moved into a senior citizens' building. She attended Bible studies, met others her age, and grew through the great teaching she received.

Our move to Riverside wasn't easy for me. I was homesick for our friends. It was during this time that I met Florence Littauer. We had much in common as speakers and our husbands encouraged us to write a seminar for women. In the Spring of 1973 Florence and I taught our first "Feminar" to only a handful of women. But it was a beginning. God was paving the way for our ministries. Florence founded C.L.A.S.S. (Christian Leaders and Speakers' Seminar), and Bob and I founded the "More Hours in My Day" seminar. Florence has written over 15 books and speaks to thousands of women all over the world. We are just two ordinary women open to God's leading, with two supportive, encouraging husbands cheering us on.

How did Bob and I grow a great marriage of 33 plus years? After all, we came from two totally different backgrounds. I was a Jewish girl raised in the city behind my mother's dress shop. Bob was a Christian young man from a farm in Texas. Only God can combine all the various elements and cause a marriage to grow tall and strong. We're still in process, but we have a great God helping grow a great marriage.

3

The Growing of a Husband-to-Be

It was planted in good soil beside abundant waters, that it might yield branches and bear fruit, and become a splendid vine (Ezek. 17:8, NASB).

Coming from a background of farmers and farming, I've always been interested in watching things grow. My grandfather, J.W. Barnes, always took great care to prepare the soil, select good seeds, plant, cultivate, water, fertilize, and finally harvest his crops. But I was also continually aware of the hardships of growing crops. I saw good years and I saw bad years. Each spring the farmers went to God in prayer, thanking Him for the past harvest—good and bad—and asking Him for a good future crop.

As a young boy I realized that being a farmer was extremely hard work. Farmers rose before sunup to milk the cows and feed the animals, then trudged off to the fields praying for good weather. Farming was the hardest work I experienced as a young man. But my goal and desire in life was to till the soil just as my father and grandfather did.

My twin brother Bill and I were born in the middle of the depression on a dirt farm outside Abilene, Texas.

My father, J.K. Barnes, was 21 and my mother, Gertie Bell Barnes, was 18. Dad was a sharecropper working for 75 cents a day with the opportunity to grow much of our food. We lived a long way out of town down a long dirt road. We had plenty of mud in the winter and dust in the summer, making it almost impossible for Mom to keep the house clean. I vividly remember catching rainwater in buckets as it dripped through our leaky roof. Some nights we would wake up soaking wet in bed from a previously undetected leak.

Bill and I weighed a total of 15 pounds at birth, and Mom weighed only 84 pounds. Due to the crowded womb, both Bill and I were born clubfooted—Bill on both feet and I on my right foot. Being poor farmers, my parents were resigned to Bill and I growing up crippled. But my grandfather heard of a young doctor who performed corrective surgery on clubfooted children. So Dad and Mom, with no money, took us to the Crippled Children's Hospital in Dallas, hoping Dr. Hodges would perform the needed surgery. God led my grandfather to assist with the finances and Bill and I underwent two years of treatments through which God healed our deformities. I am very grateful to my generous grandfather and a knowledgeable doctor. Without their help my physical development and athletic achievements would have been severely limited.

My grandfather was a very godly man who raised his family in the little white Methodist church next to the cemetery. I remember attending that church as a boy and singing his favorite hymn, "In the Garden." I still flash back to those wonderful Sunday services whenever I sing that hymn today.

In 1939 my parents moved off the farm to improve our standard of living. Dad took an eight-to-five job with the El Paso Natural Gas Company in Jal, New

Mexico, a very small town in the southeast corner of the state. In Jal I entered the first grade and my teacher, Mrs. Hulse, was a sweet, warm, and friendly lady. I've had many fine teachers over the years, but Mrs. Hulse is one of the few I remember by name.

We lived in Jal for three years. I remember coming home from church one Sunday afternoon and hearing the radio bulletin announcing the bombing of Pearl Harbor by the Japanese. Later that evening President Franklin D. Roosevelt explained the details of the attack. Most of us had never heard of Pearl Harbor, but we soon learned much about it and have never forgotten it.

The attack on Pearl Harbor played a large role in our family moving from New Mexico to Southern California. My dad's brother George worked in the oil fields in Long Beach, California. George promised Dad a good-paying job, so with little money in his pocket Dad hitchhiked to California. After two very long months, Mom and her three sons (by this time my younger brother Kenneth Eugene had been born) boarded a train to Los Angeles. At that time the trains were full of military personnel traveling from one base to another. Mom had the good fortune to meet the famous movie star Lew Ayres aboard our train as he returned to Hollywood from army boot camp. He took an interest in our family and served as our personal escort for the rest of the journey to our new state and new life-style.

In those days Hollywood was the home of the stars and we were so excited to live in the same area as Clark Gable, Lew Ayres, Gene Autry, Roy Rogers, Janet Leigh, Humphrey Bogart, Ava Gardner, Betty Grable, and many more.

Living quarters in Long Beach were hard to find during the early war years. In addition to the increased military population, Long Beach was the home of thousands who worked in several plants building planes and ships. But God was watching over our family and Dad was able to find a three-bedroom home nestled in the oil fields of Long Beach. Our rent was high at 45 dollars a month, but we were glad to have a place to live.

Long Beach was the community which shaped my identity as a young man. I obtained my education there, from elementary school through a master's degree in education from California State University at Long Beach. During my school years I was very involved in athletics, music, paper routes, student government, and church activities. I have many fond memories of those years.

When we moved to California, Mom and Dad joined Bethany Baptist Church. I vividly remember Easter Sunday in 1945 when, as a 12-year-old, I responded to the preaching of the gospel and accepted Jesus Christ as my personal Savior. I will never forget the excitement I felt after making the most important decision of my life. That night I was baptized and began my new life in Christ. Since I had been raised in the church by two very warm and loving parents, my conversion was a natural step in my growth.

As a teenager I was glad to be a Christian because I saw the Lord do so much for my relatives, neighbors, and friends. It seems like I always had good Christian models to influence me. Art Clausen, who taught a teen Bible study at church on Thursday nights, made a significant impact on my life. Our pastor at that time, Pastor Warren Glover, lifted weights at the YMCA. I was impressed that my pastor was athletic and had a good build.

During my high school years our church was very active in softball and basketball leagues. Our coach,

Lloyd Arthur, played a large role in the good direction of my life. We had some outstanding teams which won many Southern California championships in both sports. The sports program was a great outreach ministry for our church. We saw many young men come to know the Lord by attending church in order to play on our teams.

From the Easter Sunday of my conversion to September 30, 1955 when I married Emilie, my church played an extremely important role in my life. While attending this little church I began to formulate the kind of man, husband, and father I wanted to become. I'm so thankful for the many fine pastors we had. Each one made a special impression on my life. Even though I can't remember any specific sermons, I clearly remember that my pastors taught from the Bible. I began to rely on God's Word and I determined to learn it very well.

As a teenager I realized that I wanted a godly woman for a wife; one who loved the Lord as I did and who wanted to raise a family by Christian principles. I dated many girls, both Christians and non-Christians. I was looking for a girl whose heartbeat was to serve the Lord and who held solid values and goals. Up to the summer before my senior year in college I had not found the one special girl I had been praying for. I figured that perhaps God would lead me to a special girl during sorority and fraternity rush week in the fall.

One night in August my brother Bill called to ask me to repay him a favor. He told me he had met a very special girl named Esther who was staying with her friend, Emilie. Bill wanted to date Esther, but she wouldn't go out with him unless he found a date for her hostess Emilie. After several of his buddies turned him down, Bill decided that I could help him out since I owed him a favor.

Little did I know that this blind date was going to change the rest of my life. I can still remember my first impression of Emilie Klein on that warm August evening. She was real cute! She had a beautiful tan and wore a full black skirt with a white off-the-shoulder blouse. We went out for a soda and conversation after the girls' modeling class. As we took the girls home to the apartment Emilie shared with her mother and brother, I knew Emilie Klein was special. I walked her to the door and asked for her phone number because I wanted to see her again. The next day I called and we were together that evening, the next evening, and several evenings after that. I was beginning to believe that Emilie Klein was the special girl God had prepared for me.

September came and I started my senior year in college. I took Emilie to a "welcome back" party hosted by one of my fraternity brothers. That evening I learned two very disturbing facts which seemed to alter what I thought was God's direction in my life. First, Emilie was only 16, far too young for me. Second, she was Jewish, the opposite of being a Christian. At the end of the evening I told her that I wouldn't be calling her for a while because I would be very busy with my new classes.

I really thought I would meet my very special *older* girl during rush week. But two weeks passed and my special girl hadn't appeared. I told God that I was sure He would answer my prayer during my senior year— but where was she? The first football game was coming up and I didn't have a date. So I picked up the phone, called Emilie, and asked her to go to the football game with me. Her yes changed the course of both our lives. After that evening I knew she was

God's special woman for me. I wasn't sure how He was going to solve the two problems of age and religion, but I knew He could do it somehow.

One surprising answer to prayer occurred when Emilie's mother permitted her to attend church with me and my family. It was a miracle since Emilie had recently completed Hebrew school and had been confirmed in her Jewish faith. Emilie had many questions about Christ and Christianity as she heard Pastor Claude Sailhammer preach the gospel. Her questions gave me opportunities to open my Bible and give her clear, scriptural answers.

On many Sunday nights after church I parked my car in the alley behind Emilie's apartment while Emilie and I listened to Billy Graham's Hour of Decision broadcast on the car radio. I'm very thankful for Billy Graham and his ministry. He was a messenger God used to share the gospel with Emilie. One Sunday night as we listened to the broadcast we were surprised by the beam of a flashlight shining in the car window. I rolled down the window to hear the husky voice of a police officer asking, "What are you doing?" Somewhat startled, I told him we were listening to Billy Graham on the radio. "Oh, sure!" he replied disbelievingly. But after listening for a few moments, he went on his way.

One evening Emilie and I were sitting on the sofa in her living room. I held her face between my hands and looked into her eyes. I told her that I loved her very much, but I couldn't ask her to marry me. "Why not?" she asked, tears filling her eyes.

I quoted 2 Corinthians 6:14, which was deeply engraved on my heart and mind: "Do not be yoked together with unbelievers" (NIV). Then I gave her three reasons why I could not marry her.

First, a Christian cannot marry a non-Christian because of what an unequal marriage will do to the non-Christian. There is no fellowship between light and darkness. The marriage will have a divided loyalty. I said, "If I promise to marry you, I am choosing to spend my life with someone who is going in a completely different direction. We will move farther and farther apart. I have no right to draw you into a relationship which is doomed to disharmony."

Second, I couldn't marry an unbeliever because of what it might do to me. If I disobeyed God on this issue, I might compromise my standards later and disobey Him again and again. Too much was at stake if I disobeyed God's clear command about marriage.

Emilie asked, "But what if I become a Christian after we are married?" I told her that marriage is not a mission field. God never called Christians into an unequal marriage in order to convert the unbelieving partner.

Third, I said that an unequal marriage would not honor God. He did not create us and redeem us so we could live for ourselves. God placed us here to glorify Him. A Christian home is the only home which can glorify God. When a husband and wife both belong to Jesus Christ and live in obedience to Him, they provide a vital witness to the society around them.

Emilie was shocked. She had taken a very special interest in me as the type of man she could love and eventually marry. In her innocence she asked me, "How do I become a Christian?" And from that moment she began to ask herself if Jesus Christ was the Messiah her Jewish people were awaiting. After several months of seeking answers, she prayed one evening at bedtime, "Dear God: If You have a Son, and if Your Son is Jesus our Messiah, please reveal Him to me!"

Emilie expected a voice to answer her immediately. But God did reveal Himself to her within a few weeks

One Sunday morning Emilie responded to Pastor Sailhammer's challenge to accept Jesus Christ as her personal Savior. That evening she was baptized. I was thrilled! God had answered one of my two prayerful questions. Emilie had become a completed Jewish girl. Her mother didn't completely understand what had happened, but she admitted that if her daughter was happy, she was happy.

As I approached graduation and my student teaching assignments, I realized that I would soon be in the work force earning a paycheck, able to afford a wife. But I still asked God what to do about Emilie's age. Her mother surely wasn't going to give permission for her 16-year-old daughter, a high school junior, to be married. You just didn't do those things in the '50s. But I continued to pray that God would solve this problem in His own perfect way.

At this time I also developed a physical problem. The symptoms suggested the possibility of colon cancer, so my doctors began a series of tests to pinpoint the problem. During this process, Emilie's mother met a gentleman who wanted to marry her. But Irene's suitor was not sure he wanted a teenaged daughter in the arrangement. Seeing his concern, I explained to Irene that I loved her daughter, and that I would be graduating in a few weeks and able to take responsibility for a wife. "May I marry your daughter?" I asked her.

After discussing the matter with her fiancé, Irene responded, "I will be happy to give my consent for Emilie to marry you." God had finally solved the problem of Emilie's young age.

The final hurdle was my medical problem. I was to learn the test results on a Friday and, if the results proved negative, I planned to ask Emilie to marry me at a concert we were to attend that evening. When I met with Dr. Beckstrand my heart was really pounding. Many prayers had been lifted for me, so I knew God's will was being worked out for me. "You don't have cancer," the doctor announced, "but you do have a serious case of colitis." You can imagine how wonderful I felt. Now my heart was pounding with excitement. I was free to ask Emilie Klein to be my bride.

Like most couples, Emilie and I had spent many precious evenings looking at diamond rings. She had decided on a favorite and I had returned to the store later and purchased it. On Friday evening, Emilie's gleaming engagement ring, wrapped in a beautiful felt box, was hidden in my pocket as I escorted Emilie into the concert hall.

During intermission, while we were enjoying refreshments in the lobby, I summoned my courage to say, "When we get back inside I have something special to ask you."

"Oh, what is it?" she replied.

"Just wait until we are seated," I grinned.

Once back in our seats, Emilie wanted to know what was so special. "Will you marry me?" I asked shyly.

"Yes," Emilie responded confidently, "if my mother will sign for me."

"She will!" I chirped excitedly. "I've already talked to her about it!"

Almost forgetting the ring, I asked Emilie to close her eyes and hold out her hand. I pulled the box from my pocket and gently laid it on the palm of her hand. When she opened her eyes she knew what was in the box. She anxiously lifted the lid and sighed deeply when she saw the first sparkle of light from the ring. We hugged and kissed, then I slipped the ring on her finger. We decided not to stay for the last half of the concert.

Our engagement took place in April 1955 and our wedding was set for September. The months in between were filled with exciting plans and preparations. A few days before Emilie's mother was to sign our marriage license, her fiancé suffered a fatal heart attack. Irene was suddenly alone again, needing her daughter at home. But she had promised to sign and she fulfilled her commitment to us. Again God solved the problem of Emilie's age in a marvelous way.

Our wedding day began like most other days: We both went off to school—Emilie to learn and I to teach. The ceremony was scheduled for 6:00 P.M. Since Emilie's family would not come to a Christian church for the wedding ceremony, we were married in our choir director's home. Bill and Virginia Retts had been wonderful role models for us, and they graciously opened their lovely home for our small family wedding.

We can hardly remember the service, but we do remember saying "I do," kissing, and hearing Pastor Hubbard declare, "I pronounce you husband and wife." After the reception we took our gifts to our little apartment, opened them, and then headed for Laguna Beach for a weekend honeymoon.

Many people doubted that our marriage would succeed. But with helpful instruction from the Scriptures, our godly pastors, and many inspirational books, tapes, and speakers, we have succeeded to grow a great marriage. Most importantly, by allowing Jesus to be our marriage partner we have enjoyed more than 33 years together, and we look forward to many more.

Yes, our successful marriage has required a lot of hard work. The soil of our lives must be continually cultivated in order for us to bear fruit for the Lord. But as I learned from my father and grandfather during my days on a Texas farm, hard work, plenty of time, and God's blessing always produce a fruitful crop.

4

Great Marriages Need Great Wives

Her husband praises her with these words:
"There are many fine women in the world,
but you are the best of them all!" (Prov.
31:28-29, TLB).

You have already discovered that my family background was very different from Bob's. Bob grew up under an excellent model of a Christian husband—his father, J.K. Barnes. But I didn't even know what it meant to be a Christian—let alone a Christian wife—until I was 17 years old. Up to my conversion I gave very little thought to the biblical requirements for being a godly wife.

Even though I didn't know the difference between my home and a Christian home, I knew there were some problems in my family that I didn't want repeated when I married. My alcoholic father was abusive to my mother and brother, often screaming at them, swearing at them, and hitting them. For some reason Daddy never touched me, but many nights I cried myself to sleep fearing for my family and praying that Daddy would die. I knew then that I didn't want to marry a man like my father.

After Daddy died of an alcohol-induced heart attack

when I was 11 years old, our home life was better for awhile. But my brother Edmund was in junior high and soon began to test Mom's boundaries. Again our home became a battleground, this time between a rebellious teenager and a physically and emotionally weary mother.

When I was home alone I pretended that our apartment was a cute white house with a picket fence. I imagined that I was a wife and mother waiting for my husband to arrive home from work. I would clean, vacuum, and cook a delicious dinner as if for him. But often when Mom and Edmund arrived home the fantasy was shattered. Conflicts across the dinner table erupted into yelling matches which usually ended with somebody crying and doors being slammed. I would run to my bed, bury my face in my pillow, and sob, wishing I could have a normal family.

I had several girlfriends who would invite me to their homes after school to do homework and practice musical instruments. I loved being asked by their mothers to stay for dinner, and I added many of their recipes to my collection. And I really enjoyed getting to know my friends' fathers, who were always warm and friendly to me. I would go home after those visits and lie in bed thinking about my future husband and children. Happy memories from those positive families helped keep me going.

Soon after I met Bob I realized that he possessed the qualities I had dreamed about in a husband— qualities which were missing in my home. When he began taking me to his church, I discovered what God had to say in the Bible about marriage and being a wife. These truths were entirely new and refreshing to me. I became aware that God had a plan for me as a woman in His design for marriage. As Bob shared his faith in Christ with me, I could see that he had something that I wanted for my life.

Bob's family made a great impact on my life at this time. I just loved going to their home. Bob's dad was always good to me. I remember wondering if Bob would grow up to be as nice as his father. His mother, Gertie, was a great southern cook who introduced me to many new recipes. But more important than including me in their big meals, they showered me with love and made me feel like a member of the family. There were always lots of hugs, laughter, and good manners. And mealtime prayers were a wonderful new experience for me.

After several months of hearing God's Word preached and seeing it lived in Bob and his family, I came to know Jesus as my Lord and Savior. Then I started thinking about being a Christian wife. When Bob and I were married neither of us knew much of what the Bible said about being a Christian husband and wife. But we did want to learn. So we attended young married couples' Bible studies and retreats, read what we could find on the subject, and committed ourselves to be what God wanted us to be. We learned as we grew, and we are still learning to apply biblical principles to our marriage.

The Model Wife

One of the first passages of Scripture on the topic of the Christian wife which caught my attention was Proverbs 31:10-31:

> If you can find a truly good wife, she is worth more than precious gems! Her husband can trust her, and she will richly satisfy his needs. She will not hinder him, but help him all her life. She

finds wool and flax and busily spins it. She buys imported foods, brought by ship from distant ports. She gets up before dawn to prepare breakfast for her household, and plans the day's work for her servant girls. She goes out to inspect a field, and buys it; with her own hands she plants a vineyard. She is energetic, a hard worker, and watches for bargains. She works far into the night!

She sews for the poor, and generously gives to the needy. She has no fear of winter for her household, for she has made warm clothes for all of them. She also upholsters with finest tapestry; her own clothing is beautifully made—a purple gown of pure linen. Her husband is well known, for he sits in the council chamber with the other civic leaders. She makes belted linen garments to sell to the merchants.

She is a woman of strength and dignity, and has no fear of old age. When she speaks, her words are wise, and kindness is the rule for everything she says. She watches carefully all that goes on throughout her household, and is never lazy. Her children stand and bless her; so does her husband. He praises her with these words: "There are many fine women in the world, but you are the best of them all!"

Charm can be deceptive and beauty doesn't last, but a woman who fears and reverences God shall be greatly praised. Praise her for the many fine things she does. These good deeds of hers shall bring her honor and recognition from even the leaders of nations (TLB).

I have listened to others teach on this passage and

have taught from it myself for over 30 years, but I am continually learning new principles from these verses. The woman described here has been the model for my life. In fact, I have fashioned my seminar, "More Hours in My Day," from what this passage says to today's woman.

As I have studied Proverbs 31:10-31, I have identified 15 characteristics of a godly wife. I remember listing these characteristics on paper once, and then writing next to each trait ways I would develop that trait in my life. At first I thought it would be a four-to six-week project, but I have discovered that it is a lifetime assignment. I am still working on developing these godly characteristics.

The 15 characteristics are listed and described on the left below. As you read each one, jot down one or two ways by which you can incorporate it into your life (see the example for the first one).

The Godly Wife Is...

Characteristic	*Action*
1. Valuable (v. 10): She has value which increases with time.	Take a cooking class. Go back to college.
2. Trustworthy (v. 11a): She is reliable, consistent, secure; she can be counted on.	
3. Willing to satisfy his needs (v. 11b): She is understanding; she knows what makes him tick.	

Characteristic	Action
4. A helpmate (v. 12): She doesn't hinder him, but encourages and praises him.	
5. Industrious (vv. 13, 14,28): She is hard-working, diligent, active, busy, and persistent.	
6. Well-organized (v. 15): She plans ahead, shares, and gives of herself.	
7. Good in business (v. 16): She knows a good bargain and invests wisely.	
8. Energetic (vv. 17, 18): She is never lazy and often works long hours.	
9. Compassionate (vv. 19-20): She is tenderhearted, responsive, warm, and willing to help.	

Characteristic	Action
10. Domestic (vv. 21,22, 25): She is a seamstress and a designer; she is color conscious.	
11. Aware of who she is (v. 25): She has an inner peace, good self-esteem, and is physically sound.	
12. Kind (v. 26): She speaks with wisdom and kindness.	
13. Observant (v. 27): She watches what goes on and pays attention to detail.	
14. Blessed (vv. 23, 28,29): Her children bless her and her husband praises her.	
15. Spiritual (v. 30): She has the inner quality of reverence for God.	

I have met many women who didn't want to work this hard on their marriages until it was too late. Let me encourage you: Now is the time—before your marriage is in trouble—to become the person God wants you to be. And even if you are already experiencing marriage problems, it's never too late to become the person God wants you to be. Circumstances and relationships may fall apart, and perhaps they cannot be restored. But if you are open to change, God can make a new person out of you.

Recently I received the following letter:

Dear Emilie:

This is an update of my recent letter asking you for help. Evidently I have sought help too late because last Thursday my husband told me he wanted a divorce. I cannot describe the empty, sick feeling I felt at that shock. I have been barely able to eat.

I realize now my priorities were way off base. I have offended him to the point that I have destroyed God's work in his life and our family relationship. It grieves me to expose the children to this traumatic experience at their vulnerable ages.

I have asked him to let us try to work it out, assuring him that, with the Lord's will in my life, I can change. He feels it is too late. He has agreed to pastoral consultation for my benefit, but stated that his ears are closed.

Your tapes are a blessing to me at this time, but I fear that I have heard them too late.

Sincerely,

Shirley

This lady knew that her priorities were out of proper order and she was grieving to restore the damage she had caused her husband and children. Ladies, you know when things aren't right in your relationships. Please don't wait until it's too late. Confess your shortcomings to God and move into a positive position in life.

Bob uses a phrase which is a good reminder to those of us striving to be godly women: "No pain, no gain." It will cost you something to become a Proverbs 31 woman—time, energy, prayer, and discipline to name just a few. But the inestimable gain which follows the pain is the blessing and praise of your family.

The Balancing Act

Life is hectic for women today. We hear so many voices defining the changing role of wives, mothers, and women in general in society and the church. In the meantime we get tired of cooking, shopping, laundering, cleaning, ironing, and being a taxi driver taking our kids to little league games, music lessons, and church and school activities. Recently I was talking with a woman whose husband plays baseball for the California Angels. She said that, between the baseball activities of her husband and their sons, she attends up to 15 baseball games a week!

At age 21, with five children under the age of five, I was ready to give up on motherhood. I was bored and burned out. I cried, "Stop! I want off!" Sometimes when Bob was at school I would weep from frustration and fatigue. I felt like the homemaker I once read about in *The Wall Street Journal*:

THE MOST CREATIVE
JOB IN THE WORLD

It involves taste, fashion, decorating, recreation, education, transportation, psychology, romance, cuisine, designing, literature, medicine, handicraft, art, horticulture, economics, government, community relations, pediatrics, geriatrics, entertainment, maintenance, purchasing, direct mail, law, accounting, religion, energy, and management.

Anyone who can handle all those has to be somebody special. She is. She's a homemaker.

At that point in my "career" my motivations were all wrong. True, I wanted to be a helpmate for Bob, but I was caught up in the pressure of trying to meet everyone's expectations—including my own. The house always had to be perfect and the children spotless. I was frustrated as a wife and mother because I was doing it all myself—100 percent from me and nothing from God. I was trying to be the phantom wife Dennis Rainey expected his wife Barbara to be, as described in the book *Building Your Mate's Self-Esteem:*

> She is the perfect wife, mother and friend, always loving, patient, understanding and kind. She is well-organized, with a perfect balance between being disciplined and flexible. Her house is always neat and well-decorated, and her children obey the first time, every time. She is serious yet lighthearted, submissive but not passive. She is energetic and never tired. She looks fresh and attractive at all times, whether in jeans and a sweater digging in her garden or in a silk dress and heels going out to dinner. She never gets sick, lonely or discouraged. And because her phantom is a Christian, Dennis sees her faithfully walking with God daily.

> This phantom prays regularly, studies dili-
> gently and is not fearful or inhibited about
> sharing her faith or speaking the truth to
> someone who may be in error.[1]

During this time in my life I came across Philippians 1:6: "And I am sure that God who began the
good work within you will keep right on helping you
grow in his grace until his task within you is finally
finished on that day when Jesus Christ returns" (TLB).
I realized that I was the product of God working in me
and that I had three alternatives for solving my di-
lemma: First, I could continue trying to be super-wife
and super-mom by doing everything myself; second, I
could follow the old adage, "Let go and let God," and
let God do everything; or third, I could enter a balanced partnership between me and God.

I selected the last alternative knowing that, according to Philippians 2:12-13, God was at work inside me,
helping me to obey Him and to do what He wanted.
God had made me a wife and a mom on purpose, and
He would help me perform my role. Once I accepted
this truth a burden lifted from my life. I experienced
less stress and I had a better understanding of what
God wanted from me and what resources He was able
to provide for me. The drudgeries of homemaking
became a real joy when I saw myself as a partner with
God in developing godly traits in my children and
creating a warm, safe nest for our family.

As I searched the Scriptures to discover my role in
the partnership, I came up with three areas:

1. Faithfulness. According to 1 Corinthians 4:2, if
I am to be a good manager of my home, I must remain
faithful. Specifically, God wants me to faithfully thank
Him that His plans were being fulfilled in my family. I
am often impatient and want things to change "right

now." But God wants me to stop being concerned about His time-table and just give thanks that He is doing His job. Over the years I have learned that if I am faithful in giving thanks, God is faithful in His part.

2. Obedience. It is my responsibility to act upon God's promises for my life. I can't just sit back and do nothing. Nor can I wait until all situations are perfect and safe. I must do a good job of preparation and then move ahead obediently, even if it means risking failure. Some of my best steps of growth have come after failure.

3. Growth. When Bob and I attended Bill Gothard's seminar several years ago he was distributing a lapel badge with the following initials: P.B.P.G.I.N.F.W.M.Y. I was intrigued by the badge, and soon found out that the letters represented the simple message, "Please be patient; God is not finished with me yet."

Yes, the Christian walk is a process of growth. I wanted to arrive instantly at the level of being a perfect wife and mother. But God showed me that my focus was to be on the life-long process, not on arrival. If we focus on perfection we will always be disappointed because we will never achieve it. But if we focus on the process of growth we can always have hope for improvement tomorrow.

Goal Setting and Priority Planning

In Psalm 90:12 the psalmist prays, "Teach us to number our days and recognize how few they are; help us to spend them as we should" (TLB). When I read this verse I realized that God has given me only so many days to carry out His plan in my life. I decided that I needed to prioritize the various areas of my life in order to maximize my efficiency as a Proverbs 31 woman for the days God has given me.

Priority #1: God. Matthew 6:33 says: "Seek first his kingdom and his righteousness, and all these things will be given to you as well" (NIV). This verse helped me understand that, in all my responsibilities, God was to be first. He challenged me early in my married life to eliminate some of my activities and develop a deeper walk with Him.

I knew that if God was to be first in my life I needed to talk with Him more. He encouraged me to get up at 5:30 each morning for Bible reading and prayer. The early hour was difficult at first, but soon I began to enjoy getting up to talk to Him and listen to Him for 30 uninterrupted minutes.

Shortly after launching my early morning devotions, I became frustrated because I couldn't get through all my prayer requests in one morning. I needed to organize my time in order to be more efficient and effective. So I purchased a small three-ring notebook and divided the pages into the following sections for daily prayer:

Monday: Family—I keep a page for each family member, complete with a picture.

Tuesday: Church—I pray for our pastors and their families, youth leaders, elders, deacons, music director, etc.

Wednesday: Personal—I pray for my daily schedule, meal planning, cleaning, relationships, weaknesses, goals, etc.

Thursday: Finances—I pray for our budget, expenses, major purchases, credit payments, etc.

Friday: Illnesses—I pray for relatives and friends who are ill, such as Chad with chicken pox, Aunt Syd's broken hip, Bill's glaucoma, etc.

Saturday: Government—I pray for the president, governor, congress, senators, local officials, etc.

Sunday: Sermon notes/outlines—I outline each sermon and write down prayer requests from the church body to be transferred to the appropriate pages in my notebook.

For each request in my notebook I write down the date it was entered and the date it was answered. God always answers prayer in one of three ways: Yes, no, or wait. One answer from my family page has been on wait for more than 25 years. We have been asking God to give our son, Brad, a godly wife, and we will keep asking until that certain lady is revealed.

I don't get up at 5:30 A.M. these days because I now have other blocks of time for prayer which are more convenient to my schedule. One time of day is no more spiritual than another. You just need to find a block of time that is good for you. Be flexible, but be consistent.

Priority #2: Husband. One evening Bob said to me, "You love the children more than you love me. I feel like all I'm good for is a paycheck." His revelation came as a complete shock to me. He was telling me that he didn't feel needed, appreciated, or loved as he would like. I loved and respected Bob deeply, but somehow it wasn't getting through to him.

Bob's confrontation helped me realize that I was a wife to my husband before I was a mother to my children. Proverbs 12:4 states: "A worthy wife is her husband's joy and crown; the other kind corrodes his strength and tears down everything he does" (TLB). I knew I wanted to be Bob's joy and crown. I wanted to lift him up. So for awhile I focused on the area of making sure Bob was aware of his importance to me. I even helped the children invest in Dad's stock. As a team we lifted Bob to his proper position in our family.

Over the years I have assured Bob that he is a priority by mailing love messages to him, placing special "love baskets" for him to find, preparing his favorite foods, and occasionally kidnapping him for a romantic weekend. We continue our romance after more than 33 years of marriage.

If you are aware that your husband has not been a priority in your life, you may want to make special plans by which you will honor him this week. For example, you may decide to faithfully greet him at the door with a kiss or send him a love note at work.

Priority #3: Children. Deuteronomy 6:4-7 instructs us that our ministry to our children is to be a priority in our lives: "Jehovah is our God, Jehovah alone. You must love him with all your heart, soul, and might. And you must think constantly about these commandments I am giving you today. You must teach them to your children and talk about them when you are at home or out for a walk; at bedtime and the first thing in the morning" (TLB). We are to use every opportunity to teach our children about God.

We found vacation times to be an excellent time to teach our children about God and His marvelous creation. While in the desert, at the ocean, in the mountains, or beside a river we discussed God's handiwork in nature. Many times we conducted our own church services as a family with each member taking responsibility for part of the service. Vacations together were great times for us.

Another way I made our children a priority was to be available to them. As very young children they posed the most wonderful, penetrating questions. That's one of the reasons I decided to stay home with them instead of hold a job. I wanted to be there to answer their questions.

In her book, *Creative Counterpart*, Linda Dillow states: "Psychologists say the most important thing a mother can do for her child is to love the child's father, and the most important thing a father can do for his child is to love the child's mother. A child can be loved by the mother and loved by the father, but if mommy and daddy don't love each other, a child can have a deep feeling of insecurity."[2] We committed ourselves to teach our children about love by being parents who loved one another.

Your husband must be a priority over your children because eventually your children will grow up and depart, leaving the two of you alone again. If your children have been your priority, their departure may be a great shock which leaves you with many unanswered questions about your relationship with your husband. But if you have kept your husband as a priority during the child-rearing years, your love, romance, and friendship will continue to grow even in the empty-nest period of our lives.

Priority #4: Home. As a young girl I dreamed about having a home which was neat, well organized, and filled with the fragrances of cooking and baking, the sounds of soothing music, and the spoken language of love. I wanted to decorate it with frilly ribbons, bows and straw, and pictures which matched the decor. I wanted my home to be a place my friends wanted to visit.

Through the years Bob and I have been blessed to live in homes which have fulfilled my childhood dreams. But I discovered early that dreams don't make a house a home. It takes planning, organization, resourcefulness, and elbow grease to make your home a warm and welcome haven for your family and friends. That's why a godly wife "watches carefully all that goes on throughout her household, and is never lazy" (Prov. 31:27, TLB).

Even though I have a good handle on organization, I continue to be a learner in this area. I look for easier ways to complete household jobs. I read books and newspaper articles on the subject. Many of the tips I have discovered and practiced are explained in detail in three of my books, *More Hours in My Day*, *Survival for Busy Women*, and *Creative Home Organizer*.

Around our home we have annual mottoes which help keep the priority of our home in perspective. In 1986 our motto was, "Don't put it down, put it away"; in 1987, "File it, don't pile it"; and in 1988, "Do less to reduce stress." Our mottoes have been enjoyable ways to involve the whole family in caring for the home.

I challenge you to work hard to make your home an inviting place for those who live there and those who visit. Develop a decorating theme and carry it out with a flair. You don't need to be rich to furnish your home nicely. Watch for garage and estate sales, check the classified ads, and watch for sales. You can save a lot of money by patiently watching for bargain prices on the items you want.

Priority #5: Yourself. Many women come to our seminars crying out, "Does a wife and mother ever get time for herself?" Yes, but it seldom happens by accident. Priority time for yourself must be planned and appropriated.

When our children were young I found that the more organized I was in my housework, the more time I was able to carve out for myself. Also, our neighborhood mothers developed a baby-sitting co-op so that each woman could have an occasional morning or afternoon to "do her own thing."

You need to make personal time a priority to prevent burnout. Review your schedule to discover where those blocks of time for yourself may be waiting to be discovered.

Priority #6: Outside the Home. At this stage you may be saying, "I can't juggle another ball. The first five priorities already take more time than I have." If so, don't add another commitment. Each time you are asked to take an outside-the-home responsibility you have three possible responses: Yes, no, or maybe. Concentrate only on the yes responses. Wait for a different season in your life to chair the PTA, teach a Sunday school class, serve as a den mother, head up a charity fund-raising committee, or lead a women's Bible study group. Your responsibilities to God, your husband, your children, your home, and yourself are higher priorities at this time.

Leave the Changing to God

Many women I meet at our seminars ask me how they can change their husbands. I gently remind them that the Holy Spirit, not the wife, is the change agent. Our scriptural role is very clear: "Be subject to one another in the fear of Christ. Wives, be subject to your own husbands, as to the Lord.... And let the wife see to it that she respect her husband" (Eph. 5:21, 22,33, NASB). We are to reverence our husbands, not seek to change them.

Whenever I tried to change Bob, I provoked tension, discouragement, and resistance in him, and I hindered God's work in his life. Many times I found that my responses to Bob's shortcomings were worse than his shortcomings. We need to be sensitive to our verbal and nonverbal messages to our husbands, and confess our improper responses. Then we must support our husbands in prayer and be prepared to wait for the Holy Spirit to do His work.

One main reason why we want our husbands to change is because we are self-centered. We want our men to fit our ideals for the perfect husband. Instead we need to apply the wisdom of Philippians 2:3-4 to our relationships with our husbands: "Do nothing from selfishness or empty conceit, but with humility of mind let each of you regard one another as more important than himself; do not merely look out for your own personal interests, but also for the interests of others" (NASB). This is impossible to do over a long period of time without being subject to one another in the fear (reverence) of God. I continually pray for guidance in this area; Satan always wants to attack me here. And I find that this is an area where most women are vulnerable.

Instead of changing your mate, you need to concentrate on what God wants from you. First Peter 3:1-2 tells women how to live with an unresponsive mate: "Wives, fit in with your husbands' plans; for then if they refuse to listen when you talk to them about the Lord, they will be won by your respectful, pure behavior. Your godly lives will speak to them better than any words" (TLB). Is this easy to do? Not until you come to grips with the fact that God designed marriage relationships to work best this way.

Wives, God wants us to respect our husbands. Maybe he doesn't deserve your respect, but that doesn't matter. Linda Dillow says: "God does not say your husband has earned the right to be your head or deserves it. He says that He, God, decided this was the best plan and therefore asks you to honor the plan."[3] Speak respectfully of him in private and in public, and teach your children to do the same. Accept him at face value and trust God for any needed changes. Submit to his authority in God's chain of command (see 1 Cor. 11:3). Build his self-image by showing approval and admiration. I have found Dennis and Barbara Rainey's book, *Building Your Mate's Self-Esteem*, to be a helpful resource in this area.

Greet your husband at the door with a hug and a kiss. Tell him you are glad he is home and give him space to unwind and adjust from work and the freeway to home. Tell him you love him in many creative ways. Step out of the way and let him take the lead God ordained for him. Don't continually nag, remind, belittle, or embarrass your husband. Aim for that quiet and gentle spirit that will prompt your husband to say, "There are many fine women in the world, but you are the best of them all!" (Prov. 31:29, TLB).

5

Great Marriages Need Great Husbands

> Husbands, love your wives, even as Christ
> also loved the church, and gave himself for it
> (Eph. 5:25, KJV).

When Emilie and I entered our joint union with
Jesus in 1955, we did so without the benefit of Christian marriage seminars, or books and tapes by Dr.
James Dobson or Chuck Swindoll. All we had was the
Bible, a wise pastor, and the counsel of our families
and Christian friends. So we stepped into married life
leaning heavily upon these resources.

When it came to learning how to be a good husband, I had a good role model in my father. Dad was a
God-fearing man who wanted to do what the Scriptures taught. His generation had even less teaching
in the area of family life than I did. But Dad's example
provided some valuable lessons which got me off to a
good start.

For example, Dad loved his wife—something my
brothers and I never worried about or doubted for one
moment. Dad was always bringing Mom flowers and
an occasional box of candy, kissing and hugging her in
front of us, and even giving her secret little pinches
when he thought we weren't looking.

Furthermore, Dad took his family to church. He was not one to drop us off and return home to drink another cup of coffee and read the Sunday paper. No sir! He was the leader of our spiritual pack Sunday morning, Sunday evening, and Wednesday evening for prayer meeting. Dad prayed at our meals, prayed alone, and read his Bible faithfully. He was a deacon or trustee for many of his years, and he regularly gave of his money and his time to the church. I am grateful to God for the example of a spiritual husband and father He provided for me in my dad.

Sadly, many men today enter into marriage with little or no positive role models from their past. And often new believers have little knowledge of the scriptural guidelines for the husband's role in marriage. This generation of Christian husbands is bombarded with opportunities to learn these truths through Christian marriage seminars, videos, tapes, and books. Yet we still find many men asking, "What is my role in marriage?"

Sometimes the husband's role is clouded by the unrealistic expectations his wife brings into the relationship. Barbara Rainey, co-author with her husband of *Building Your Mate's Self-Esteem*, describes the phantom husband she projected on Dennis:

> He rises early, has a quiet time reading the Bible and praying, and then jogs several seven-minute miles. After breakfast with his family, he presents a fifteen-minute devotional. Never forgetting to hug and kiss his wife good-bye, he arrives at work ten minutes early. He is consistently patient with his co-workers, always content with his job, and has problem-solving techniques for every situation. At lunch he eats only perfectly healthful foods. His desk is never cluttered,

and he is confidently in control. He arrives home on time every day and never turns down his boys when they want to play catch.

His phantom is well-read in world events, politics, key issues of our day, the Scriptures and literary classics. He's a handy-man around the house and loves to build things for his wife. He is socially popular and never tires of people or of helping them in time of need. He obeys all traffic laws and never speeds, even if he's late. He can quote large sections of Scripture in a single bound, has faith more powerful than a locomotive, and is faster than a speeding bullet in solving family conflicts. He never gets discouraged, never wants to quit, and always has the right words for every circumstance. He also keeps his garage neat. He never loses things, always flosses his teeth and has no trouble with his weight. And he has time to fish.[1]

Men, as hard as we might try, we probably won't be able to fulfill all of our wives' expectations for us, especially if they are as lofty as Barbara Rainey's. But we do have a standard to shoot for which, if diligently pursued, will help us to honor God and please our wives. Let's turn to God's Word and see what He has to say on the important topic of the husband's role in marriage.

The Submissive Husband

In his letter to the church at Ephesus, Paul gave some profound instruction on how we are to serve Christ in our various relationships. A key verse on this topic is Ephesians 5:21: "Be subject to one another in the fear of Christ" (NASB). This verse really caught

my eye because it comes *before* the specific instructions to wives and husbands beginning in verse 22.
The first instruction to husbands and wives is to adopt
a spirit of mutual submission to one another out of
reverence for Christ. A Christian husband and wife
each have Christ living in them. In order to reverence
Christ we must reverence the vessel He dwells in.
When we submit to one another we are submitting to
Christ. That's the only way verses 22 and 25 can make
sense. Without an attitude of mutual submission the
husband becomes the big boss and the wife becomes
the doormat. But the priority of mutual submission
keeps the specific instructions to husbands and wives
in proper perspective.

Paul teaches husbands about their role in Ephesians 5:25-30:

> Husbands, love your wives, just as Christ
> loved the church and gave himself up for her
> to make her holy, cleansing her by the wash-
> ing with water through the word, and to
> present her to himself as a radiant church,
> without stain or wrinkle or any other blem-
> ish, but holy and blameless. In this same
> way, husbands ought to love their wives as
> their own bodies. He who loves his wife
> loves himself. After all, no one ever hated
> his own body, but he feeds and cares for it,
> just as Christ does the church—for we are
> members of his body" (NIV).

My first response to this instruction was, "Oh, that's
easy—as long as she promises to love me first, wash
my clothes, cook great meals, and always look pretty."
Then I remembered verse 21 and reminded myself

that I can't act on the basis of such promises. Loving Emilie had to start with submitting to her and to the Lord. Once I grasped that principle I began to submit to Christ in a fresh, new way. Even though Ephesians 5:22 states that Emilie was to be submissive to me, I knew I was subject to a higher calling—*mutual submission.* I began to realize that I was not to control or dominate Emilie, but I was to humbly and sacrificially love her. I was to set aside my rights and serve her needs.

Fortunately I was raised in a home which taught and modeled sacrificial love through kindness and good manners. So during our courtship I graciously opened the car door for Emilie, assisted her with her chair when being seated at the dining table, allowed her to go through the doorway ahead of me, and performed other kind acts I had learned as a boy. But Paul's instructions helped me see that the motivation for such kindness to Emilie was humble submission to Jesus in her.

I heard a true story about a man whose wife had always wanted him to open the car door for her. But instead of complying he would always make fun of her request with remarks like, "What's wrong with your own two hands? Are they broken?" And he refused to open the car door for her.

The man's wife passed away before he did. At her funeral he was preceding the pallbearers as they carried her casket to the hearse. Since the man was the first to arrive at the hearse, the funeral director asked him to open the door so the pallbearers could slide the casket inside. As the man reached for the door handle he remembered his wife's persistent request. He sadly realized that the only time he had fulfilled her wish was at her funeral.

Through all the years of our marriage I have always opened the car door for Emilie. My practice must have caught on with our children because our son, Brad, does the same for his dates. Several of his girlfriends have commented that Brad was the only gentleman who would open the car door for them. When our daughter, Jenny, and her husband, Craig, were first dating, Jenny told Craig that she would like him to assist her with the car door. Craig, who was also raised to practice good manners, was glad to accommodate her request.

At first glance manners may seem to be a small area of submission. But manners are a very practical way to show our reverence for Christ by serving our mates.

Submissive Leadership

Another area where I learned submission was in my role as the leader in our home. I didn't want to impose my will on Emilie by demanding that she do what I say. I found that when I led out of respect for Christ and for my wife, Emilie was eager to follow.

Through the years of our ministry we have found that women are eager to follow their husbands' lead in attending church, praying and reading the Bible together, giving, attending couples' retreats, etc. Our wives are just waiting for us to take responsibility for spiritual leadership in our homes. Our children are also looking for spiritual direction and leadership. They feel more secure when we place boundaries around them. Recently our daughter, Jenny, said to me, "Dad, I thought you were too strict when Brad and I were growing up. But now I appreciate the direction you provided for our lives. Craig and I are going to be even tougher on our three children."

Jesus does not lead the church as a harsh dictator. He leads by taking initiative, by loving, and by serving. This is the pattern of leadership we men need to follow in leading our families. Take a few moments right now to jot down some steps of leadership you need to put into motion in these three areas:

Taking Initiative	Loving	Serving
1.	1.	1.
2.	2.	2.
3.	3.	3.

They say it takes 21 days to establish a new habit. Stick with your new steps of leadership until they become second nature. And remember: Your goal is not to change your mate; it's to change you. Ask yourself, "Would I like being married to me?" If you cannot answer with a wholehearted yes, what changes do you need to make in you? List some of them here:

Changes in Me

1.

2.

3.

4.

I would like to tell you that our marriage has always been heavenly, but I can't because it hasn't.

Great Marriages Need Great Husbands

Whenever I strayed from the instructions in Ephesians 5:25-30, I have experienced marital problems. No, we have never talked about getting a divorce; the word has never been in our vocabulary. When I committed myself "for richer or for poorer, in sickness and in health," I meant it. However, there were times when my pursuit of success wrongfully took priority over my growth as a Christian. I put God on hold for several years. We didn't stop going through the motions of a wonderful family. But in my heart I knew that I wasn't the spiritual husband and father I was supposed to be.

My turning point was in 1967 when we moved to Newport Beach, California and began attending Mariner's Church. At that time I got involved with a group of men who began to challenge me to fulfill my role as a Christian husband and father. I experienced a new awareness that my first responsibility after serving God is to serve my wife. I have endeavored to fulfill that responsibility ever since.

Unconditional Love

We were standing in line at the airport one morning waiting to board a plane taking us to the site of one of our seminars. I noticed a man and woman ahead of us in line who were obviously saying their last good-byes before he boarded our plane while she stayed behind. They were kissing and hugging very affectionately, acting like newlyweds. All the while he was facing us and her back was toward us.

Finally, after a long kiss and embrace, he boarded the plane while she lingered at the gate waving good-bye. By this time I was very curious to get a look at this woman. The couple was so much in love, and I wanted to see what she had going for her. I took a long gaze as we moved past her to enter the gate, and I was astonished. Her face was severely disfigured, marred by jagged scars. Tears came to my eyes as I realized the depth of the man's love for such an unfortunate woman. I was touched by his willingness to show his affection openly despite her obvious handicap. It was an example of unconditional love I shall never forget.

Our submissive, serving love for our wives is to be unconditional, committed to giving, not getting. The focus is to be her heart's desires, not ours. Consequently I can never view my wife as an instrument of my pleasure or convenience such as my nurse, servant, dishwasher, cook, errand girl, etc. I can never ask her to do something degrading or harmful in order to fulfill my whims or wishes. She is my helpmate and my partner. We are a team with similar goals and desires. I must continually love her and serve her for who she is, not what she can do for me.

The Responsible Husband

Another passage of Scripture which has given me direction for my role as a husband is 1 Peter 3:7: "You husbands likewise, live with your wives in an understanding way, as with a weaker vessel, since she is a woman; and grant her honor as a fellow-heir of the grace of life, so that your prayers may not be hindered" (NASB). Peter clearly states here that husbands must perform two responsibilities and, in return, will receive one specific reward.

Responsibility #1: We are to live with our wives in an understanding way. The King James Version of 1 Peter 3:7 says we are to "dwell with them according to knowledge." Knowledge of what? The knowledge of wives and marriage, of course. As Tim Timmons says in his Maximum Marriage seminars, we need to find out why wives are weird and husbands are strange.

The only formal training in family life I had prior to marriage was a course in high school called, "Senior Problems," and it taught me practically nothing about living with a wife. I never read a book or magazine on the subject, and I had very few conversations with my father or my pastors on the subject. I had no married buddies who could tell me how to dwell with my wife according to knowledge.

Learning to live with our wives in an understanding way is more on-the-job training than anything else. Seminars, books, and tapes are great, but there is no substitute for patient, observant, day-to-day living with a wife to expand your knowledge of her. Even in my fourth decade with Emilie I am still learning about her. Our marriage relationship is always in process. In my role as a knowledgeable husband, I keep coming back to an encouraging little saying which is etched in my mind: "I am not what I am going to be or what I want to be, but I thank God that I'm not what I used to be."

What are some areas you want to better understand about your mate and your marriage? Write some of your questions below, then decide on how you will start finding the answers to each:

Questions I Have   **How I Will Find Answers**

1.   1.

2.   2.

3.   3.

4.   4.

5.   5.

Responsibility #2: We are to grant our wives honor as fellow-heirs of the grace of God. The dictionary defines honor as an act that shows respect or high regard. One of the ways we can honor our wives is by being respectful and courteous, and by employing good manners, as we have already discussed. Another way to honor them is by openly communicating our appreciation for who they are and what they do. Tell your wife that you like her new hairstyle, that you enjoyed the recipe she tried for dinner, that the house looks neat, or that the children are responding well to her training. Thank her for ironing your shirts and fixing your sack lunches. Express your appreciation in conversation, in notes and cards, and in special treats like dinner out or a getaway weekend.

Honor your wife by speaking favorably of her to others. She is not your "old lady." She has a name, and she has accepted the role of being your wife and the mother of your children. Your respectful words about her will fulfill Ephesians 4:29 by edifying all who hear you. We must also teach our children to honor their mothers with respectful talk and behavior. If children are discourteous or impolite to their mothers, they will carry the problem into their marriage relationships by being disrespectful to their mates.

Peter described our wives as fellow-heirs of the grace of life. That means that our wives are to be equal recipients of the gifts God has for us. The current women's liberation movement is 2,000 years behind the times. God gave women a position of spiritual equality when He gave us the New Testament. I know that many husbands are threatened by their wives' spiritual growth. But my prayer over the years has been that Emilie would become the woman that God wants her to be. I am not threatened by her growth or her spiritual gifts, even in the areas where she outshines me.

The honor we show our wives is like an investment, such as the investments Emilie and I have made in stocks, bonds, mutual funds, certificates of deposit, and treasury bonds. Over the years we have watched our stocks increase in value and enjoyed the dividends which our investments have returned. Similarly, as you invest daily in your wife by honoring her in word and deed, you will see her sense of self-worth increase. Furthermore, you will reap dividends in your marriage which greatly exceed your initial investment.

The reward: Our prayers will not be hindered. Peter suggests that our relationships with our wives correlate directly to our relationship with God. If you fail to understand and honor your wife, your prayers will be hindered; but if your horizontal relationship with your wife is in harmony, your vertical relationship with God will also be in harmony. You cannot ignore God's principles for marriage and expect to grow in your relationship with God.

List below what you are already doing to fulfill each responsibility. Then list a few areas where you are lacking and what you can do to improve those areas:

Understanding My Wife

I Am Doing	I Am Lacking	I Will Do
1. Showing kindness	1. Patience	1. Practice patience
2.	2.	2.
3.	3.	3.

Honoring My Wife

I Am Doing	I Am Lacking	I Will Do
1. Compliment her	1. Courtesy	1. Open car door
2.	2.	2.
3.	3.	3.

The Manager in the Home

As Emilie and I travel the country speaking in seminars, we hear a lot of women asking this question: "How can I get my husband involved in the home? He is so passive." It is clear to us that many Christian husbands have not accepted the spiritual responsibility of being the leaders in their homes.

First Timothy 3:1-13 contains a list of specific qualifications which Paul instructed Timothy to look for in church leaders. But I believe any man who is seeking God's will in his life should use this list as a guideline whether or not he is a pastor, elder, or other church leader. The qualifications here outline. the characteristics God is looking for in all Christian men.

Look particularly at verses four and five: "He must be one who manages his own household well, keeping his children under control with all dignity (but if a man does not know how to manage his own household, how will he take care of the church of God?)" (NASB). As a former school principal and owner of a manufacturing company, I know what the word "manage" means. A manager presides over and leads those he is responsible to manage. Christian husbands are the God-appointed managers of their homes. It is important that we fulfill our scriptural role by taking leadership in the home. Emilie began to respect taking leadership in the home. Emilie began to respect me more when she saw in me the desire to be the manager of our home.

In his book, *Christian Living in the Home*, Jay Adams gives an excellent explanation of the husband's role as the manager of the home:

> A good manager knows how to put other people to work.... He will be careful not to neglect or destroy his wife's abilities. Rather he will use them to the fullest.... He does not consider her someone to be dragged along. Rather, he thinks of her as a useful, helpful and wonderful blessing from God.... A manager has an eye focused on all that is happening in his house, but he does not do everything himself. Instead, he looks at the whole picture and keeps everything under control. He knows everything that is going on, how it is operating, and only when it is necessary to do so steps in to change and to modify or in some way to help.[2]

During the 1950s when Emilie and I were married, husband and wife roles were much more clearly defined. In those days the husband took care of everything outside the house and the wife concerned herself with everything inside the house. We heard phrases like: "That's not my job"; "I'm not changing the diapers—that's a mother's job"; "The yard needs mowing—Dad and the boys will do it." Fortunately Emilie and I did not contract our marriage on that basis. I had seen my father do many jobs around the home that were considered "woman's work." So I had no problems helping with the dishes, changing diapers, baby-sitting while Emilie went to the market, ironing my own shirts, and even doing the laundry occasionally.

Also during the '50s the man of the house was to write the checks and control the purse strings. We were warned that it was almost unchristian for the wife to pay the monthly bills. But I couldn't go along with it. I had a wife who was very good at finances. We established a budget together for our fixed expenses and decided together where to spend our spending money. Since Emilie was so good with numbers, I asked her to write the checks. This was difficult for her at first because she thought I needed to be responsible for our finances. But for over 25 years she has written the checks after we have decided together what needed to be paid. My job has simply been to manage.

Of course, not all wives may be gifted in finances like Emilie is. Perhaps the husband is better equipped to write the checks and keep the books. I've even heard of families which have delegated the finances to capable teenagers. What an excellent way to teach a child financial responsibility!

Today the guidelines for management in the home have changed drastically. Gone are the days when the fathers went to work and earned the money while the mothers stayed home to take care of the children. The working mother is now a staple in the work force. We recently met a retired man who stays home to cook delicious meals and keep house while his wife maintains a job outside the home. They love their new roles.

Not long ago Emilie and I ran into a former co-worker of mine in a grocery store. I asked about his family and he said that he quit his job to stay home and raise the children. His wife was so successful in her computer career, and making so much more money than he could make, they had decided to reverse roles. He loved his duties at home and she loved her career much more than homemaking.

As these examples suggest, managing today's home and family is a responsibility which can be delegated in a number of ways. Each family is unique and free to decide what arrangement works best for them, even if it is different from any other family. The most important concern is that you weigh the variables unique to your family and establish a plan. As the biblical managers of our homes, we men are responsible to see that a plan is put into action. We may not always be right and we may need to change the plan from time to time. But it is our responsibility to lead our families in establishing, evaluating, and modifying plans of action which effectively meet the needs of our wives and children.

The greatest enemy of the successful husband/manager is passivity. We tend to want to lay back and let things happen instead of step forward and make things happen in our homes. We cannot yield to the temptation to abandon our God-given role. We must get on with the program. When we do, our wives and our children will have greater respect for us.

The biblical pattern for the husband's role in managing the home is found in 1 Corinthians 11:3: "Now I want you to realize that the head of every man is Christ, and the head of every woman is man, and the head of Christ is God" (NIV). The chain of command is clear: God above Christ, Christ above man, man above woman. This principle is often difficult to maintain in our culture, but if we are to survive the attacks on the family today we must return to God's manual on the subject and follow His plan. When you accept the role of a responsible manager, and carry it out with the heart of a servant, your family will flourish.

6

Growing Together Despite Differences

> By wisdom a house is built, and by understanding it is established; and by knowledge the rooms are filled with precious and pleasant riches (Prov. 24:3-4, NASB).

Emilie and I encounter many women attending our seminars or seeking counseling who are plagued by disquieting concerns and questions about their relationships with their husbands. We hear comments like these all the time:

- ❧ My husband says he's tired of talking at work and just wants to relax when he comes home. Why won't he talk to me?
- ❧ My husband doesn't spend any time with the children and he expects me to handle all the discipline. How can I get him to take some responsibility?
- ❧ My husband blames me for a messy house, but he won't clean up his mess. Are all husbands this sloppy?
- ❧ My husband works late at the office and golfs on Saturdays. We never see him at home. Why doesn't he enjoy family life as I do?

- ❧ My husband never makes a decision; he wants me to decide. He says his job is all he wants to think about.
- ❧ My husband is always depressed. What can I do about it?
- ❧ Why do I get the feeling that my husband wants me to be his mother instead of his wife?
- ❧ My husband is rarely romantic, and never shows his emotions. Why?
- ❧ My husband tells our sons to be tough and to fight for their rights. I disagree with him, but he says that's the way boys should be.

Similarly, a lot of men catch our ear with their complaints about their wives:

- ❧ I don't mind talking when I get home from work, but for two hours?
- ❧ My wife has spoiled the children all these years and now she wants me to discipline them.
- ❧ My wife has nothing to do all day but take care of the house, but it's always a mess when I come home. What's she doing all day?
- ❧ I try not to go home early after work or be home during weekends. With the wife and kids home there's nothing but confusion—loud voices, doors slamming, and everything lying around in a mess.
- ❧ I won't decide where the family is to go on an outing anymore because, when I do, nobody wants to go there.
- ❧ My only source of depression is that I don't make enough money or own a prestigious job title which meets my wife's approval.

❧ My wife wants me to be romantic and huggy all
the time. But I can't waste my time doing that
when I've got so many other things to do.

❧ My wife wants to make sissies out of our boys.
She wants them to take piano and dance lessons, but I want them to be football players.

It's evident to Emilie and me, as it should be to
every husband and wife, that men and women are
different—even beyond the obvious physical differences. And these differences are the root of our problems as couples. Marital friction is not so much from
husbands and wives being physically, emotionally,
psychologically, and culturally different, but that we
don't understand our differences and accommodate
them in our relationships.

In order to have a growing marriage, we must have
teachable hearts to learn how God has designed husband and wife to be different and complementary.
Some men and women have the false impressions that
the opposite sex thinks and reacts the same way they
do. Nothing could be farther from the truth. Our goal
in this chapter is to identify the ways in which men
and women are different so we can better understand
ourselves, our mates, and our need to complement
each other.

Physical Differences

Physical differences are not the most prominent
differences which cause relationship problems between husbands and wives. But God did make us
different physically, and these differences must be
understood in the blending of two lives. Let's look at

some of the physical differences between men and women:

- ❧ About 130 males are conceived for every 100 females conceived. But only 105 males are born for every 100 females born.
- ❧ Women live an average of eight years longer than men.
- ❧ Men are usually stronger than women and able to run faster and lift greater weights than women.
- ❧ Women are immune from some diseases which affect men.
- ❧ Men produce XY chromosomes; women produce XX chromosomes.
- ❧ The presence of the hormone testosterone in men increases their tendency toward aggression and physical activity.
- ❧ Men lose weight faster than women due to the lower ratio of muscle to fat.
- ❧ Men have a higher metabolic rate than women.
- ❧ A man's blood gives off more oxygen than a woman's.
- ❧ Women have greater endurance over the long haul than men, and can maintain a level of energy longer than men during the day.
- ❧ A woman's capacity to exercise is reduced two percent every 10 years, whereas a man's capacity is reduced 10 percent over the same period.
- ❧ Men are performance-oriented in sexual intercourse; orgasm is the goal. Women are more interested in closeness and communication in sex, and they will trade physical sex for being held, caressed, and talked to.
- ❧ Men must be physically aroused for sex; women don't need physical arousal.

Psychological Differences

Men and women are also different psychologically—in the construction of the brain and the way it works. Dr. Joyce Brothers, in her book, *What Every Woman Should Know about Men*, states:

> The fetus has what scientists call a "bipotential and undifferentiated brain," which means it can go either way (male or female) depending on the influence of sex hormones. The brain is divided into a left and right hemisphere. The left (the verbal brain) controls language and reading skills. We use it when we balance our checkbook, read a newspaper, sing a song, play bridge, write a letter.... The right hemisphere (intuitive brain) is the center of our spatial abilities. We use it when we consult a road map, thread our way through a maze, work a jigsaw puzzle, design a house plan or plan a garden.[1]

Doreen Kimura elaborates on the differences between the male and female brain in her article from *Psychology Today*:

> Sexual differences in the way the brain is organized suggest different ways of thinking and learning. The male brain is specialized. He uses one side for solving spacial problems, the other side for defining a word or verbalizing a problem. The female brain is not so specialized for some functions such as defining words. A woman's right-brain and left-brain abilities are duplicated to

some extent in each hemisphere and work together to solve problems.[2]

This data on right-brain and left-brain leads us to several observations regarding the psychological differences between men and women:

❧ Women can better sense the difference between what people say and what they mean.

❧ Women are more perceptive than men about the meaning of feelings.

❧ Men have difficulty understanding women's intuition, often thinking that women are too sensitive.

❧ Women are more perceptive than men about people.

❧ Men and women think differently and they approach problem-solving differently. Men are more analytical and deal with the problem more objectively. Women personalize and personally identify with the problem.

❧ Women can work on several thoughts or projects at one time. Men want to concentrate on only one thing at a time.[3]

Cultural Differences

Physical and psychological differences between men and women have given rise to several cultural differences. Sometimes it is difficult to tell where the unlearned hormonal differences leave off and the learned cultural differences begin.

In his book, *Why Men Are the Way They Are*, Warren Farrell states that men are performers who must have an acceptable level of production to feel self-fulfilled. As a performer he is competitive and goal-oriented. As an initiator he is vulnerable to risk and failure, so he is defensive in his relationships—even with his wife. Long-term relationships are risky for a man because he tends to expose his weaknesses, making him vulnerable to greater hurt and possible defeat. That's why men are more apt to leave their marriages than women. Instead of growing close to his woman, a man will defend himself from hurt and defeat by escaping the relationship. If he doesn't stay very long, his wife cannot hurt him and thus prove him to be a failure at the performance of marriage.

A man's insurance policy against failure in his relationships—especially his marriage—is to succeed in business. He rationalizes that if he is successful in the working world he can buy whatever he needs to raise his self-esteem and self-worth to a level he can live with, even if he is not successful on the home front. Success at work protects him from the pain of his failure at home.[4]

A man's pursuit of success often produces characteristics which make him unlovable at home. When I was working on my master's degree and trying to get a mobile home business off the ground, I was not always pleasant to live with around Emilie and the children. Emilie thought I should value the things she valued: home life, child-raising, etc. But I was busy— perhaps too busy at times—making my mark on the world as all men must do. Emilie did not always understand my unique need for success and approval on the job.

There are many other assumed cultural distinctives which men feel they must live up to in order to be real men. While most of these are on the fringes of credibility, they must be confronted in the marriage relationship to avoid some obvious problems:

❧ The man is the breadwinner in the family. If your wife works, you are less than a real man.

❧ Men don't quit until they are carried off the field.

❧ Being "macho" is important. You must be in shape, wear the right clothes, drive the right car, and be a member of the right country club.

❧ Men must know about "men things": Boats, trucks, planes, cars, sports, etc.

❧ Men always read masculine magazines and never look at women's magazines.

❧ A man can perform sexually under any condition, and do so several times.

While a man is task- and success-oriented, his wife is basically relationship-oriented. When a man comes home after a busy day, he has already accomplished what he feels is really important—winning the battles at the shop, office, or store, and providing for his family. He wants to relax, watch TV, and read the paper. But his wife is excited that he is home and she wants to talk. He's ready to kick back, but she's ready to kick into gear. She's waited all day for him to come home so they can relate.

Women sincerely want their men to express deep feelings and thoughts, to listen to them, and to try to understand a wife's emotions. A woman wants to be more than a nurse, cleaning lady, and cook to a man on his way to the top. She wants to share in her man's life. She wants a relationship based on communication and intimacy.

In her book, *In a Different World*, Carol Gilligan summarizes the tension in the male-task versus female-relationship difference: "Since masculinity is defined through separation while femininity is defined through attachment, male gender identity is threatened by intimacy while female gender identity is threatened by separation. Thus, males tend to have difficulty with relationships while females tend to have difficulty with individualization."[5]

In addition to the primary cultural differences of task- and relationship-orientation between men and women, there are several other cultural differences—often framed from childhood—which shape our role expectations in marriage:

- ❧ Blue is masculine and pink is feminine.
- ❧ Boys are supposed to be big, tough, and active, while girls are small, cute, and pretty.
- ❧ Boys should play with trucks, boats, guns, and trains, while girls should choose dolls.
- ❧ Mothers are more affectionate with girls than boys. Boys are more fussy than girls, and girls sleep better than boys.
- ❧ Boys are trained to be independent and girls are trained to be compliant.
- ❧ Boys are competitive and girls are cooperative.
- ❧ Boys collect in small groups and gangs; girls are more adept at one-on-one.
- ❧ Men play softball and tell war stories; women have tea parties with intimate conversation.
- ❧ Girls pattern themselves after their mothers; but boys don't want to copy feminine traits because they fear they will look like sissies around other boys.[6]

We find ourselves in a transition period in our culture regarding the roles of men and women. Our western culture is still very masculine in nature and emphasis. Our boys and men are taught to be tough, yet more and more they are encouraged to be tender.

They learn early to take risks and take control, but their wives urge them to be vulnerable and transparent. Men generally feel more secure in mirroring traditional roles, but they are finding that today's woman needs a sensitive, caring man more than a Mr. Macho.

As men become more firmly established in the traditional male roles, they become more hostile in rejecting the female role.

Created Differently

Men and women are different in many ways, including physiology and anatomy, thought patterns, and cultural roles and expectations. For the most part, these differences are the result of God's design. Genesis 2:27 reads: "And God created man in His own image, in the image of God He created him; male and female He created them" (NASB). And Psalm 139:13-14 states: "Thou didst form my inward parts; Thou didst weave me in my mother's womb. I will give thanks to Thee, for I am fearfully and wonderfully made" (NASB). In these two passages we get a glimpse of God's marvelous plan in human creation. Men and women, as different as they are, are made in God's image. God called this creation good, and David remarked that it was wonderful. A Christian husband and wife can move into their marriage relationship with the confidence that God has put each on the earth for a special purpose. Our differences are by God's design.

In Matthew 22:37-39, Jesus outlined simply and directly the greatest commandment in the Scriptures: "You shall love the Lord your God with all your heart, and with all your soul, and with all your mind" and "You shall love your neighbor as yourself" (NASB).

This command provides the primary guidelines for responding to our differences as husband and wife.

First, we are to love God. This implies that we accept His creation as good and agree that the male-female differences He designed are good. Second, we must love ourselves. This means you must accept yourself for what God has made you: a unique man or woman created for a special and different purpose than your mate. Third, we are to love others, particularly the mates God gave us—complete with their differences. Loving our mates doesn't mean changing them—that's the Holy Spirit's role. Loving our mates means understanding their differences and accepting them as they are. I think that is one of the lessons of Proverbs 24:3-4: A loving understanding of one another as husband and wife establishes our house. Seeking to understand one another is a continuous process which leads to less anger and frustration in the relationship. We still may have difficulty with each other's actions, but at least we are growing in the understanding of why our mates do what they do.

Another scriptural guideline for dealing with differences in our marriages is Romans 12:2: "Do not be conformed to this world, but be transformed by the renewing of your mind, that you may prove what the will of God is, that which is good and acceptable and perfect" (NASB). The world teaches us to stand up for your individuality and not to give in to accommodate your mate's differences. But Paul directs us not to conform to that standard, but to be transformed by the renewing of our minds. We are to let God's teaching on the blending of differences permeate our thinking and, subsequently, our acting.

As Christian men and women, we are, and ever will be, different. As we take God's attitude toward our differences we will enjoy a house "filled with precious and pleasant riches" (Proverbs 24:4, NASB). These rewards are positive attitudes, good relationships, pleasant memories, mutual respect, and depth of character. We have a choice. We can live in a war zone fueled by our differences as men and women. Or we can live in a house filled with the precious and pleasant riches which come from understanding and accepting our differences.

Perhaps the greatest enemy of understanding and accepting differences is pride. God hates pride, yet we seem to struggle against it in everything we do, especially us men. We must break down the walls of pride which our differences erect in order to enjoy the rewards which understanding promises.

Delightfully Different

Emilie and I have experienced the entire gamut of differences discussed in this chapter. Not only were our backgrounds different, but we have dealt with all the classic physical, emotional, and cultural differences during our marriage. But there has never been an air of competition between us. We have always wanted to complement each other. We are committed to Christ and to the foundation of the Christian home to make our relationship work. I am committed to love Emilie as Christ loved the Church, and she is dedicated to be my helpmate and to reverence me as her husband. With these points of agreement we are able to surmount our differences, and, in response to our prayers, God is able to use us to His glory in spite of our differences.

Our marriage of more than 33 years has been typical in our roles and expectations of one another. I was oriented to masculine endeavors, job satisfaction, and goals, and Emilie has been slanted toward relationships. In all fairness, I've had to make more adjustments to move away from worldly conformation. I was locked into the macho-tainted expectations which characterize other men. I had tunnel vision regarding the home, children, God, and church. I had to open myself to moving in a godly direction instead of accepting the worldly attitude which was all around me. I had to overcome the barriers of pride, distrust, and suspicion in our marriage to accept our differences and occupy my scriptural role.

Romans 12:2 played a large part in alerting me not to be conformed to the world's role for a husband, but to be transformed to God's way of thinking about marital roles. I realized that if Emilie and I were going to survive marriage and family life, I needed to shatter the worldly mold which threatened to conform me to its shape. I had to search the Scriptures to discover that we were both made for the purpose of worshiping and enjoying God. We had each been wonderfully created with unique male or female characteristics. We weren't to be abrasive to one another in our differences. Rather we were to allow God to develop each of us to complement the other according to His plan. By studying Ephesians I was able to look at marriage afresh and to understand God's design for this institution. Every question regarding our differences was answered by Scripture; I just had to study it and apply it.

While I was discovering my scriptural role in the home, Emilie was growing too. God was preparing her to share with other women what she was learning about the wife's role in marriage. As each of us got to know God better through studying His Word, we got to know each other better. Gradually our differences and inadequacies became less effective instruments in Satan's attempt to neutralize our marriage and our ministry.

One of the most helpful tools in our development as husband and wife was the book, *The Spirit-Controlled Temperament,* by Dr. Tim LaHaye. As members of the Mariner's Church in Newport Beach, California, Emilie and I attended a couples' retreat at Forest Home Christian Conference Center which featured Tim and Beverly LaHaye as speakers. We got excited about the new information we received explaining how husbands and wives are different because of their temperaments. We highly recommend this book to you as you work through your differences.

Several years later we were exposed to the ministry of Florence Littauer. Using the LaHayes' teaching on the temperaments, Florence helped us to examine our own personal strengths and weaknesses, and then to accentuate the positive and eliminate the negative. Furthermore, she helped us understand that people who are different from us, including our spouses, are not wrong—just different. Once we examine ourselves and stop trying to change others, we open our own hearts to change. When we realize that others can be different without being wrong, our relationships improve. God created each of us to be unique. The variety of natures and differences between us adds spice to life as each of us sees the same events from a different point of view.[7]

The second half of Romans 12:2 states: "Be transformed by the renewing of your mind, that you may prove what the will of God is, that which is good and acceptable and perfect" (NASB). Yes, you have a choice. You can be conformed to this world or transformed to God's point of view. We know hundreds of couples who have chosen the latter alternative. We recommend, with them, that you stop living in the war zone of your differences and allow God to lift you to new heights in your relationship in spite of your differences as man and woman.

Emilie and I have found that our differences have led to a richer and more meaningful relationship, not only for ourselves, but for all the people we contact and minister to through our seminars. May God also be with you as you begin to appreciate your individual differences. And may your differences actually become elements of cement in your relationship, giving new life, spice, and adventure to your marriage. As we often say, don't compete—complement!

7

You Can't Grow if You Don't Communicate

Dear brothers, don't ever forget that it is best to listen much, speak little, and not become angry (Jas. 1:19, TLB).

Marriage experts tell us that the number one cause for divorce in America today is a lack of communication. Everyone was born with one mouth and two ears—the basic tools for communication. But evidently possessing the physical tools for communication is not enough. Couples must learn how to use their mouths and ears properly for true communication to take place. Since God created marriage for companionship, completeness, and communication, we can be sure that He will also provide us with the resources for fulfilling His design.

There are three partners in a Christian marriage: husband, wife, and Jesus Christ. In order for healthy communication to exist between husband and wife, there must be proper communication between all three partners. If there is a breakdown in dialog between any two members, the breakdown will automatically affect the third member of the partnership. Dwight Small says: "Lines open to God invariably open to one another, for a person cannot be genuinely open to God and closed to his mate.... God fulfills His design for Christian marriage when lines of communication are first opened to Him."[1] If you and your mate are having difficulty communicating, the first area to check is your individual devotional life with God.

Whenever Emilie and I suffer a breakdown in relating to one another, it is usually because one of us is not talking with God on a regular basis. When both of us are communicating with God regularly through prayer and the study of His Word, we enjoy excellent communication with each other. As Diagram A suggests, the closer Emilie and I get to God, the closer we grow together as a couple. The inverse principle is also true: The farther we move away from God by not communicating with Him, the farther apart we will be from our mates.

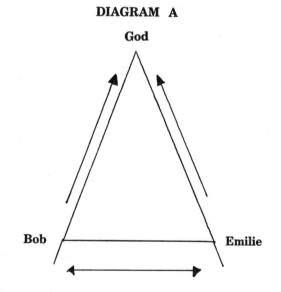

DIAGRAM A

Diagram B illustrates a similar principle by using a cross. The vertical line represents our relationship to God and the horizontal line represents our relationship to others, including our mates. If the horizontal relationships are shaky and about to collapse, it is usually because our vertical relationship to God is weak.

DIAGRAM B

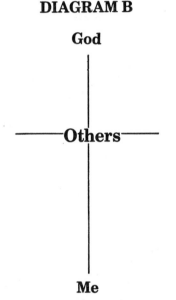

God

Others

Me

What Is Communication?

In his book, *Communication: Key to Your Marriage*, Norm Wright gives an excellent definition of communication: "Communication is a process (either verbal or nonverbal) of sharing information with another person in such a way that he understands what you are saying. *Talking* and *listening* and *understanding* are all involved in the process of communication."[2]

According to Wright, there are three elements in proper communication: talking, listening, and understanding. Let's look at each of these in detail.

Talking

Most of us have little difficulty talking. We are usually willing to give an opinion or offer advice, even when it hasn't been requested. Often our communication problems are not from talking, but from talking too much.

James 3:2-10 states that the human tongue can be employed for good purposes or bad. The tongue is like a rudder which can steer us into stormy or peaceful life situations. From experience we know that our mouths can say wonderful words in one moment, and in the next say something hurtful or embarrassing. First Peter 3:10 warns us to keep control of our tongues. We must watch our mouths at all times and be continually alert to its positive and negative capabilities.

Solomon said: "A word aptly spoken is like apples of gold in settings of silver" (Prov. 25:11, NIV). Teaching on this passage, Florence Littauer says that our words should be like silver boxes tied with bows. I like that description because I can visualize husbands and wives giving lovely gifts like silver boxes to each other in their conversation. In Ephesians 4:29, Paul gives us another lesson in proper speech which we can apply to our communication with our mates: "Let no unwholesome word proceed from your mouth, but only such a word as is good for edification according to the need of the moment, that it may give grace to those who hear" (NASB). We are not to speak ugly words which tear down our mates, but we are to speak uplifting and encouraging words that will bring a blessing.

Sometimes our verbal communication is best accomplished in writing. Make sure your family members get your messages clearly by leaving notes on the bulletin board, on the counter, or by the telephone. Emilie and I like to leave notes of encouragement in unusual places to lift up one another: in a lunch sack, suitcase, or briefcase, or under a pillowcase. We've even used a water-based felt marker to write messages to each other on the tile inside the shower stall. After being read the message can be easily washed off.

A card or letter sent through the mail seems to be more enthusiastically received than a note left out to be found. Everybody likes to get good mail. Sometimes homemade cards are a lot of fun to make and send.

Listening

Listening is a skill which most people haven't learned. Of Wright's three elements of communication—talking, listening, and understanding—listening is usually the trouble area. Instead of patiently hearing what our mates have to say, most of us can hardly wait until they stop talking so we can put in our two cents' worth. God gave each of us two ears, but only one mouth. Consequently we should be ready to listen at least twice as much as we speak.

Listening is the disciplined ability to savor your partner's words much like you savor and enjoy a fine meal, a thoughtful gift, lovely music, or a great book. To properly listen is to take time to digest the content of the message and to let it get under your skin and into your system. When we openly and patiently listen to our mates, we truly learn from them. The following questions will help you probe your personal listening attitudes and habits:

1. Have you already stopped listening? In some couples, one or both partners have already stopped listening to the other. They block out everything their mates say by hiding behind a newspaper or working long and late. If you find yourself shouting at your mate to be heard, you are probably married to someone who has stopped listening.

When your mate stops listening to you, you will probably react by either withdrawing and talking less or overcompensating and talking louder and longer. Neither reaction is productive in the long run. If your mate is not listening to you, it may be because you are not communicating at a level which invites your mate's participation. In his book, *Why Am I Afraid to Tell You Who I Am?* John Powell lists five levels of communication, each one deeper and more meaningful than the last. Try to identify the level you and your mate most commonly employ, then seek to improve your communication by moving to deeper levels.

Level five is *cliché conversation*, which includes everyday, casual conversation based on safe, surface statements like, "How are you?" "How's your family?" "Where have you been?" "I like your suit." Lacking in depth, cliché conversation barely acknowledges that the other person is alive.

Level four is *reporting the facts about others*. At this level you are quoting others instead of giving personal commentary: "It will be a sunny day"; "The Orioles lost their twentieth straight game"; "The score of the football game was 17-6." There is little or no emotion or commitment at this level.

Level three, *my ideas and judgments*, is where real communication begins. Here you are willing to step out and risk expressing a personal opinion in order to be part of the decision-making process. You may feel insecure at this level, but at least you are willing to take a chance. Persons who are threatened at this level often retreat to the higher levels of communication.

Level two is *my feelings, my emotions.* At this level we express how we feel about the facts, ideas, and judgments expressed at higher levels. We may say, "I feel so much better when the sun is shining." Information is not enough at this level. Feelings must be shared in order to communicate.

Level one encompasses *complete emotional and personal truthful communication.* This level of communication requires complete openness and honesty, and involves great risk. All deep and enriching relationships operate at this level. It takes a great deal of trust, love, and understanding to communicate truthfully. This level is not a dumping ground, but a place where each partner treats the other with love and concern.[3]

Use the following questions to help you evaluate the present communication level in your marriage:

> What level of communication is most common to you and your partner?
>
> What are the indicators of your communication level?
>
> What actions can you take to move your communication to a deeper level?

If you as a couple have stopped listening to each other, here are some helpful tips we have learned about listening which you should take to heart:

- ❧ Realize that each of you has a basic need to be listened to.

- ❧ Listen intently when your partner is talking to you. Don't just think about your answers. Listening is more than politely waiting your turn to speak.

- ❧ Listen objectively. Put down the newspaper, turn off the television, look your partner in the eye, and pay attention.

- ❧ Reach out and care about what is being said. Listening is active participation, not passive observance.

- ❧ Move past the surface message and get to the heart of what is being said. Listening is more than hearing words.

- ❧ Discipline yourself to listen. Listening doesn't come naturally or easily to any of us. Most of us are more comfortable when we are in control and speaking.

- ❧ Receive and process the message sent. Try to understand what is being said. At times the message may be painful, but you will be stretched if you continue to listen.

Timing is an important element in the success of communication. Honor your mate by selecting the best times to talk, listen, and understand. Emilie always allowed me the first 15-30 minutes after I arrived home from work to unwind. We didn't bring up difficult topics at that time unless there was an emergency. We reserved mealtimes for pleasant, edifying, and uplifting conversation. Serious topics were

saved until after the pangs of hunger had been satisfied. Then, between dinner and bedtime, we covered
more serious issues.

If you have a very serious topic to address, you
might want to secure a baby-sitter and invite your
mate out to dinner so you can talk away from the
distractions at home.

2. Do you presume or judge as you listen? As a
father, I can recall many times when our children
would come to me asking permission to do something
or to go somewhere. Often I would start shaking my
head no before they would finish asking their questions. This was a great disservice to them because I
was telling them their opinions and requests were
unimportant before they had time to fully express
them. The answer may still have been no, but they
would have accepted and understood better if I had
listened to their requests, discussed them, and then
given my answer.

Proverbs 18:13 says: "What a shame—yes, how
stupid!—to decide before knowing the facts!" (TLB). In
order for our mates and children to realize that we
value their input, we must thoroughly hear them out
before giving a response or pronouncing a judgment.
This is especially important when the subject under
discussion is of little interest to you. As a husband you
must welcome the news of your wife's day, particularly
when the children are young. Words like diapers,
doctors, shots, crawling, mess, and nerves all have
meaning to your wife. If they are important to her,
then they must become important to you, even if they
have little meaning to you.

We made it a habit to take our children with us
when we looked for a new home, new car, sporting
equipment, stereo, and other items of family interest.
We wanted them to give us input on these purchases,

and we disciplined ourselves to listen to their comments acceptingly. Many times their suggestions proved to be very helpful in our final selections. But they never would have given them if we hadn't carefully listened to them.

3. Do you touch when you listen? Touching is probably the best way to tell your mate that you are listening to him or her. The amount of encouragement and affirmation which can be communicated through touch is astounding. Often no words are needed when there is a hug, a hand clasp, an arm around the shoulder, or even a playful pinch. Sometimes your mate just wants to be held or caressed assuringly. They are crying out, "Are you listening? Do you care?" Your touch assures them that you are in tune with what they are saying.

4. Are you a gut-level listener? Gut-level listeners are intense listeners. They focus beyond what their mates *say* to hear what their mates *mean*. They are open and compassionate, asking in-depth questions and ready to communicate at level one on Powell's list. Without gut-level listening we often miss the real meaning of the words being spoken. We must learn to listen more with our heart and soul than with our ears.

5. Do you take time to listen? Communication doesn't happen by itself. You must plan for it and spend both quality-time and quantity-time doing it. If you don't have time for your mate and your children you are too busy. C.R. Lawton said, "Time is the one thing that can never be retrieved. One may lose and regain a friend; one may lose and regain money; opportunity spurned may come again; but the hours that are lost in idleness can never be brought back to be used in gainful pursuits." And time spent listening to our mates and our children is time well spent.

We cherish a letter we received from our son, Brad, while he was in college. It reads:

Dear Mom and Dad,

As I sit here studying for my finals, I need to take a break and write you a note to express how much I appreciate the time you have given me over the years. I would not be here studying in college if it wasn't for you giving your time to encourage me along the way. As I think about the money you invested in my college education, I am aware of the many hours that Dad had to work to provide this time in my life.

I remember back to elementary school when you both always attended my school's open house, many times after you had already spent a long day at work. You both took me down to the City Council one evening when I received the award for being the best athlete at East Bluff Park. I also remember you taking me down to the fire station to teach me a lesson after I set fire to my mattress while foolishly playing with matches. I know you weren't happy about that, but you were there.

Remember all the swim meets, and the little league games that lasted until 10:00 P.M.? It got cold and foggy some evenings, but you were both there cheering me on until the last out.

In junior high you were there with your time and car to take my first girlfriends to school functions. There were more ball games, tournaments, long trips, cold bleachers, sweaty gyms— but you were there.

You really gave a lot of time in high school— attending ball games, transporting me to school and church activities, and sponsoring my youth groups. You were even at the car wash when only a few students showed up, washing and drying cars until you were so tired at day's end. Both of you attended booster club meetings after the football games to catch a glimpse of me on the films making a good catch or tackle.

College wasn't much easier on your schedule. You took time to write me, phone me, and visit me. Parents' weekends at the fraternity house were great with you there. My friends really liked that you were with me. They think you're great! Many of their parents didn't find the time to visit on those weekends. I guess they were too busy, but you weren't. Thanks for all that. You were there.

Yes, Mom and Dad, you always gave me time, but the best thing I remember you giving me was your prayers and godly advice. Many times I could have gone astray, but with each opportunity I looked around and you were there. I will always appreciate the time you gave me. I only hope that one day I will be able to return the favor by giving my wife and children the time you so graciously gave me.

Well, it's time to get back to my marketing notes. I love you both very much.

Love, Brad

Yes, there were many evenings that Emilie and I would have rather been doing something other than attending a ball game or an open house. But a long time ago we decided that our kids were more important than other activities. Now we are glad we made that commitment of time to our kids. We realize what a blessing they are.

You will either give your time now or later to your kids. If you don't take time to listen to them and care for them now, you will be forced to spend time picking up the pieces of their insecure lives later.

Understanding

While vacationing in Mexico recently we went into a neighborhood restaurant for dinner. Our waiter didn't speak English very well, but he wrote our order on his pad, then looked us in the eye and said, "*Si.*" We were sure he understood our order because of his affirmative response. However, when he returned with our dinner—or what he thought we had ordered for dinner—we couldn't help laughing at the missed communication.

We may speak clearly and our mates may listen intently, but if they don't understand the message, we haven't communicated very well. There are two major reasons why we fail to communicate this way. First, when we speak there is often a difference between what we mean to say and what we really say. The idea may be clear in your head, but the words you choose to express the idea may be inappropriate.

Second, when we listen there is a difference between what we hear and what we think we hear. Perhaps the words you heard correctly conveyed the speaker's idea to everyone else, but you misunderstood them. And every time you respond to what you think you heard instead of what was actually said, the communication problem is further compounded.

One way to help clarify your communication is to repeat to your mate what you heard, and then ask, "Is that what you said?" Whenever you stop to ask that clarifying question you are helping to keep the channels of understanding wide open and flowing. If Emilie is reporting an event to someone in my hearing, and says it happened at five o'clock when I thought it happened at six o'clock, I will immediately ask, "Five o'clock or six o'clock?" When it's all said and done, does it really make a difference if all the facts are told right? Usually not! That's why "Five o'clock or six o'clock" has meant so much to us.

How to Communicate Better

In her book, *After Every Wedding Comes a Marriage*, Florence Littauer reviews what men and women are looking for in communication. Being aware of your mate's general needs in this area will help you better communicate with him or her.

According to Littauer, men want four things: (1) Sincerity—They want to know that the topic is important to you; (2) Simplicity—They want to hear the simple facts and get to the point; (3) Sensitivity—They will open up better at the right time and the right place; and (4) Stability—They want to keep their composure and not fall apart during communication.

Women have four different wants: (1) Attention—They want their mate's full attention when they speak; (2) Agreement—They want no arguments to break down the walls between them and their mates; (3) Appreciation—They want their mates to value them and their role; and (4) Appointments—They want their mates to honor the time and place for communication.[4]

Let me share a few additional tips that Emilie and I have successfully applied to our communication as husband and wife:

1. Be willing to change. If you have been guilty of hindering communication in your family, you are not locked into that behavior. Ask God and your family members to forgive you for your failure. Then learn from your mistakes and change your communication pattern. Tomorrow is a new day.

2. It's okay to disagree, but not to disrespect. Always maintain respect and honor for your mate when communicating your differences. Don't belittle, slander, or attack your partner, even in a heated exchange.

3. It takes effort to communicate well. When you decide to communicate better, be aware that your decision is only the beginning. It takes a lot of effort from both partners to grow as good communicators. Communication is a matter of will and work.

4. Don't second-guess your partner. Sit on your hands, keep you mouth shut, and hear your partner out, even if it takes several hours for him or her to communicate.

Solving Communication Breakdown

There are many reasons for communication breakdown between partners—perhaps as many reasons as there are couples. But there seem to be several problems which afflict many couples. Maybe you will recognize some familiar communication problems in your marriage from the list of statements below:

> I am afraid you will laugh at me.
> I know my opinion doesn't matter to you.
> I am afraid of your reaction.
> I talk so much that you stop listening.
> I know you will correct me or prove me wrong.
> I get too depressed to talk sometimes.
> I get angry too easily when we talk.
> I don't like serious conversations so I make jokes when we talk.

I am afraid of the silence between us.
I don't like it when you interrupt me.
I am afraid we won't agree.
I am afraid you will make fun of me or my
  ideas.
I always feel defensive when we talk.[5]

If you and your mate want to prevent or repair communication breakdown, you must identify the problem areas and plan a program to overcome them. In some cases the barriers to communication may be so great that you need to seek a trained Christian counselor. Until the barriers are broken down you will never be able to respond to your mate properly.

Following the example in space number 1, list some of your real or potential communication barriers below on the left. Then determine some actions you will take to prevent or repair each problem and write your ideas on the right:

Communication Problems	Actions for Improvement
1. I am afraid of your reaction.	1. Take the risk to pray about my approach. Choose the right time and share how I feel when he/she talks about a difficult situation.
2.	2.
3.	3.

4.   4.

5.   5.

Christian marriage and family counselor Norm
Wright says that many of us don't communicate because we don't believe that Christ accepts us as we
are. And since we don't feel accepted by Christ, we do
not accept ourselves, and we cannot accept others and
communicate with them. We are too busy trying to
shape up for God so that He will love us and accept us.

The good news, of course, is that God has already
accepted us because of our relationship to Jesus Christ.
We don't need to prove anything to Him. We simply
need to accept His love and reflect His love by accepting ourselves and others. Acceptance opens all the
doors which lead to communication.

As I mentioned at the beginning of the chapter,
communication between Christian marriage partners is a spiritual exercise. The closer you each get to
God, the closer you can get to each other. Perhaps you
are not communicating well as a couple because you
have never opened the lines of communication between
yourselves and God. Each of you must initiate the
conversation with God by asking Him to come into
your life in the person of His Son Jesus Christ. Then
seek out a church where you can grow in your relationship to Christ. As your communication with God
blossoms, you will enjoy increasingly better communication with each other.

8

Growing into Great Sex

> Let marriage be held in honor among all,
> and let the marriage bed be undefiled (He-
> brews 13:4, NASB).

Our society is bombarded with it from the cereal boxes we see in the morning to the moisturizing lotions we use at night. We see it everywhere we look—from magazines to newspapers, from radio to television, from the advertising on gigantic billboards to the advertising posted on the sides of city buses. Billions of dollars each year are spent by manufacturers using it to persuade you and me to purchase their products. The "it," of course, is sex. Everywhere we turn we are confronted with sexy women and lusty men who are trying to influence us by promising that a certain brand of car, underwear, toothpaste, or soft drink will fulfill our needs for love, sex, and intimacy.

In Emilie's background, sexual intimacy was synonymous with a dull, dirty duty. Her home, dominated by a violent alcoholic father, was anything but a model of romantic love, fulfilling sex, or warm intimacy between a husband and wife. According to Emilie's early view, sex was something a couple did to have children. It was not something which was pleasurable or enjoyable.

When her father died, Emilie was left without a father figure for the important teenage years of her life. So she came to our marriage without a healthy understanding of the role of love, sex, and intimacy between a husband and wife. She was first attracted to me by the gentleness and warmth which she had missed in her home. But she had no positive model from home as a point of reference for developing intimacy in our relationship.

Contrary to Emilie's experience, I was brought up by very warm, gentle, loving parents. There were always positive expressions of love and intimacy around our home. Sex was much more to our parents than creating children. It was a topic which was discussed with high respect. My parents were very open with their hugs, kisses, compliments, and playful pinches. They started their romancing early in the day and were ready to show the world how much they loved each other.

So on the topic of love, sex, and intimacy, Emilie and I were examples of the axiom that opposites attract. We entered our marriage relationship from two opposite poles—as different as hot and cold. And yet here we are—well into our fourth decade together as husband and wife, and more in love now than when we started. I could have "rushed and crushed" Emilie with my sexual warmth and openness, and she could have iced our relationship from her background which lacked intimacy. But with love, trust, and patience on both our parts, our relationship has grown into the warm, loving, intimate, and sexually fulfilling partnership we enjoy today.

God thought up the idea of marriage and human sexuality. "And the Lord God said, 'It is not good for man to be alone; I will make a companion for him, a helper suited to his needs' " (Gen. 2:18, TLB). I am so thankful to God that He gave me a helper like Emilie. He knew that I should not be alone and He made Emilie just for me. Our differences in background may suggest that God made a mistake in bringing us together. But He made no mistake. He knew Emilie was perfectly suited for my needs. Over the years she has truly been the perfect companion and helper.

Love, sex, and intimacy are important parts of a marriage relationship. In this chapter we want to share some insights which have helped us succeed in this vital area.

Intimate Differences

As a young man of 22, I thought that boys and girls were alike in their approach to love and sex. First came physical attraction leading to marriage. After marriage came sexual fulfillment. Then from sexual intimacy true love developed. But when I married Emilie I learned that women don't approach love the same way. I soon found out that what Emilie desired most in marriage was love, not sex. She desired sexual fulfillment too, but for a woman sex is more a by-product of love. Whereas a man grows in his love for his wife through sexual fulfillment, a woman finds greater sexual fulfillment when she is assured of her husband's love.

Men can usually function sexually on the basis of eroticism and physical stimulation alone. A man can become erotic at a selfish level with any woman who is sexually available. It is easy for a man to engage in sex outside of love.

Women, on the other hand, generally are more emotionally-oriented. Though they are capable of being intensely erotic, a woman usually responds sexually to a man who provides her with security, understanding, tenderness, and compassion. Women who have extra-marital affairs usually do so because they are angry, lonely, insecure, or generally unfulfilled in their marriage relationships.

As a healthy, red-blooded male, my love for Emilie was first physically-oriented. I expected that she, like me, was easily aroused sexually and that the sex act was a primary focus for her. But when I realized that she placed more value on love, affection, and the feelings of romance, I had to slow down and make sure I was fulfilling those needs for her. When I learned to assure Emilie of my love for her in nonsexual ways, sexual fulfillment came more easily for both of us.

Developing Intimacy

Many women have reacted angrily against their husbands who have become workaholics, refusing to spend quality time with their wives. When our wives are lonely or unfulfilled because we don't spend time with them, they will be less likely to respond positively to our sexual advances. Dr. Kevin Leman's book title, *Sex Begins in the Kitchen* (Regal Books), captures the idea. Men, don't wait until bedtime to start getting romantic. Set the stage at breakfast with kind words and loving touches. Leave a thoughtful note, give her a call during the day, greet her at the door with a hug, a kiss, a wink, and a listening ear. She needs more than your sexual prowess to fulfill her; she needs you!

A primary way to develop intimacy is through the language we use in our communication. Emilie and I have always tried to express our love by using positive language with each other. One of our key verses on this topic is Ephesians 4:29: "Let no unwholesome word proceed from your mouth, but only such a word as is good for edification according to the need of the moment, that it may give grace to those who hear" (NASB). We have made a point of trying to encourage and uplift each other in our speech.

One of the ways we have filled our speech with love is in the careful choice of words we use with each other. We like the two lists Denis Waitley shares in his book, *Seeds of Greatness*, indicating words we should forget and words we should remember in loving conversation:

Words to Forget	Words to Remember
I can't	I can
I'll try	I will
I have to	I want to
I should have	I will do
I could have	My goal
Someday	Today
I can't	I can
I'll try	I will
I have to	I want to
I should have	I will do
I could have	My goal
Someday	Today
If only	Next time
Yes, but	I understand
Problem	Opportunity
Difficult	Challenging
Stressed	Motivated
Worried	Interested
Impossible	Possible
I, me, my	You, your
Hate	Love[1]

Are there some words in your communication you need to forget and replace with words which affirm your love and deepen your intimacy? Consciously watch your language and be sure to communicate by using positive, loving words. If your words are not edifying, switch gears in your mind and your mouth, and begin to speak only words to remember.

Once the lights are out, men, slow down and be patient. Tell your wife that you love her and talk to her lovingly. Take time for plenty of foreplay with gentle caresses, hugs, and sweet words. Then after intercourse, allow time for more talking and tenderness, and assure her further of your love for her. Sexual intercourse may happen in the bedroom, but fulfilling lovemaking begins hours and sometimes days earlier.

And women, it's okay for you to assume the giver's role in sexual intimacy at times. For many years it has been the man's role to initiate lovemaking. But God gave women the desire for sex too, and there will be times when she will be the initiator in intimacy. Some of our most exciting romantic evenings together have been planned by Emilie. She prepares our traditional "love basket"—a large basket lined with lace and filled with favorite foods, sparkling cider with two tall glasses, a candle, and even a bunch of fresh flowers. The setting can be a picnic in the park or at the beach, at an outdoor concert, or beside a stream. The gourmet love basket meal can even be served in the bedroom by candlelight with soft music playing. There is a complete chapter on the love basket in Emilie's book, *More Hours in My Day*.

Wherever we go, Christian couples ask us, "Is it okay for Christian couples to . . . ?"—and they finish the question with a variety of sexual practices. We usually refer to the verse which begins this chapter, Hebrews 13:4: "Let marriage be held in honor among all, and let the marriage bed be undefiled" (NASB). Emilie and I have used this verse as a guideline in determining what we would incorporate in our intimate loving. We talk to each other to see if the activity in question is something that would enrich our intimacy. If we agree that we would both enjoy and profit from the activity, we feel free to do it.

Sometimes a couple will put certain lovemaking techniques on hold because one partner is uncomfortable with the idea. You must be very sensitive to your partner's desires in these areas and must not get too far ahead of him or her. If you aren't sure about certain practices, apply the principle in Proverbs 3:6: "In all thy ways acknowledge him, and he shall direct thy paths" (KJV). Talk to the Lord together about the activity. It's amazing how God will reveal the proper answer for you when you need an answer.

Sexual fulfillment is the result of meeting each other's sexual needs. We are to be students of our mates in order to be able to meet their needs. What better way to learn than to ask questions and discuss feelings, needs, and expectations. In their book, *Bedroom Talk*, David and Carole Hocking state: "Both partners should be committed to bring sexual pleasure and complete satisfaction to each other. We have found a good way to approach this subject with your mate, and we hope it helps you. Simply ask the following questions: 1. Is there anything you would like me to do for you sexually that we are not doing now? 2. Is there anything you do not want me to do?"[2]

Loving questions like these eliminate assumptions and pave the way for deeper intimacy and greater fulfillment in sex. When Emilie tells me where she likes to be touched and stroked, I can more completely meet her needs and enrich our lovemaking.

Alternate the roles of giver and receiver in foreplay and intercourse. Don't get into a rut. Keep some mystery in your sex life. The sex act alone without daily romantic encounters, communication, and mutual contentment can become shallow and lonely. We need to help each other through verbal and nonverbal communication to express our wants and preferences to each other. Love is more than sex. But sex in the context of total love is rich and fulfilling.

God's Idea of Intimacy

The Bible's teaching on marriage has really helped Emilie and me to realize that God has a master plan for husbands and wives. One of the most important passages we have discovered is 1 Corinthians 7:1-5:

> It is good for a man not to touch a woman. But because of immoralities, let each man have his own wife, and let each woman have her own husband. Let the husband fulfill his duty to his wife, and likewise also the wife to her husband. The wife does not have authority over her own body, but the husband does; and likewise also the husband does not have authority over his own body, but the wife does. Stop depriving one another, except by agreement for a time that you may devote yourselves to prayer, and come together again lest Satan tempt you because of your lack of self-control (NASB).

There are four principles in these verses which provide solid guidelines for couples who desire love and intimacy in their relationship:

1. Be faithful to one person. Sexual immorality was rampant in the society surrounding the Corinthian church to which Paul wrote. Our society today hasn't progressed very far from that low level. Christian men and women today are often tempted to moral failure in their places of employment and many fall to the affections of a coworker. But God warns each of us to confine our affections to one person—our own spouse—and no one else.

2. Be available to each other. Each husband is to give himself to fulfill the needs of his wife, and each wife is to give herself to fulfill the needs of her husband. We are to freely ask for and give affection to one another. Don't be afraid to tell your mate that you are in the mood for love, and always be ready to respond when your partner is in the mood. If you find that you are too tired to fulfill each other's needs and enjoy each other, maybe you need to eliminate some other commitments and activities in order to comply with this scriptural directive.

3. Submit to each other. Your role is to be sensitive to your partner's needs and willing to meet those needs at all times. If your mate wants to make love, you should not withhold yourself from him or her, but submit to his or her desires. Be aware that your willingness to meet your partner's sexual needs and desires may very well prevent him or her from falling into moral sin with someone who is more ready to meet his or her needs than you are.

4. Keep on doing it. The only exception to continually meeting each other's sexual needs is during a time when you agree together to withhold yourselves from each other for the purpose of prayer and fast-ing. Other than at these specified times, a husband and wife should be each other's continual sexual servants—always seeking to meet each other's needs.

In order to promote an atmosphere of love and mutual fulfillment, we need to foster romance in our marriages. Are you a romantic husband or wife? If not, start sending flowers and making phone calls to say, "I love you." Leave sexy notes for each other and send thoughtful cards expressing your love in tender words. Give your mate physical attention: Hold hands, touch tenderly, hug and kiss often. If your mate comes from a home which is less affectionate than yours, patiently grow together as physically romantic partners by lovingly teaching each other the magic of touch.

Love in Three Dimensions

In our culture love is often equated with physical attraction, sexual feelings, and the act of intercourse. Love in this narrow context is selfish, mainly desiring that the love object meet personal needs. But love in the Scriptures involves attitudes and actions which are aimed at meeting your mate's needs irrespective of your personal feelings.

In his book, *The Measure of a Marriage*, Gene Getz defines three Greek words which encompass the selfless three-dimensional love which should be present in our marriages:

Erao love. Erao refers to sexual love. Though the word is not found in the New Testament, it was used during New Testament times to describe sexual activity which was based on selfish, sensual, erotic lovemaking. It's the kind of love most frequently displayed in today's movies, books, and magazines. *Erao* always involves a sexual response.

Christians may not feel that *erao* has a place in the sanctity of a Christian marriage. But erotic experiences, within the bounds of faithfulness to one's spouse, is an important part of marital love. For the Christian, erotic lovemaking must always be expressed within the boundaries of *agape* and *phileo*.

Phileo love. Phileo refers to love that is emotionally positive in nature. It reflects true friendship, delight, and pleasure in a relationship. Romans 12:10 states that we are to be devoted to one another in brotherly love. *Phileo* describes the type of loving relationship which exists among family members: devotion, support, commitment, affection. *Phileo* is the dimension of love which involves responding to someone's needs affectionately and with positive emotions. Husbands and wives must learn to be devoted friends as well as lovers.

Agape love. Agape is the most common word for love in the New Testament. It is love which actively seeks to do the right thing for, and meet the needs of, the love object. It is love which sacrifices personal feelings and needs to meet the needs of the spouse. In *agape* we willingly give up our rights, our desires, and our demands to fulfill our partners. You may come home from work too tired to be kind or romantic to a spouse who needs your loving attention. But *agape* loves beyond what we feel like doing. *Agape* patiently seeks to discover and meet the needs of the other no matter what the personal cost may be.[3]

The diagram on the next page illustrates that all facets of love must reside within the boundaries of *agape* love. Our goal as Christians is to allow *agape* love to penetrate and rule the other two dimensions of love in our lives. In order to allow *agape* its rightful place, you must first know Jesus Christ as personal Savior and be submissive to your spouse. If you

Three Dimensions of Biblical Love

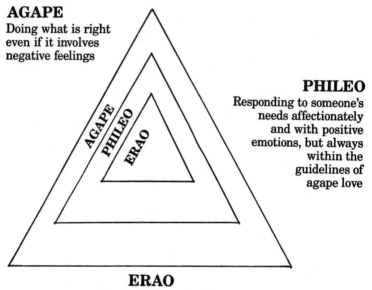

AGAPE
Doing what is right
even if it involves
negative feelings

PHILEO
Responding to someone's
needs affectionately
and with positive
emotions, but always
within the
guidelines of
agape love

ERAO
Becoming emotionally,
physically, and
sexually involved with
another person, but
always within the
guidelines of agape
and phileo love

haven't made these basic commitments, you cannot move beyond *erao* and *phileo* love. Many marriages can survive on these two dimensions of love alone, but it is God's will for Christians to allow *agape* to dominate all their relationships, especially marriage.

Feelings of Intimacy

The feelings which develop in a relationship guided by *agape* should be positive and not negative. Feelings are often a barometer which reveals how well we are doing at developing the intimacy we seek in marriage. The following lists contrast positive and negative feelings which can accompany a relationship. You can use these lists to evaluate your progress in developing intimacy in your marriage. Place a check to the left of each feeling which is present in your life, positive and negative. Add some words of your own to the lists if necessary:

Positive Feelings	Negative Feelings
Pleased	Anxious
Understanding	Fear
Hopeful	Lonely
Tenderness	Uncertainty
Proud	Insecure
Closeness	Confusion
Excited	Sad
Happiness	Rejection
Contented	Angry
Confident	Bored
Acceptance	Helplessness
Grateful	Scared
Affectionate	Frustrated

Sexual arousal	Frigidity
Eager	Foolish
Elated	Confused
Calm	Apathetic[4]

Now take some time to think about some of the negative feelings which need to be changed to positive feelings in your relationship. List below on the left some of the negative feelings you checked. Then decide on one action you could attempt for each to turn it into a positive feeling:

Negative Feelings to Change	**Positive Actions to Take**
1.	1.
2.	2.
3.	3.
4.	4.
5.	5.

Intimate Tips for Men

What kind of man is best suited for intimacy in his relationship with his wife? I suggest that it is the man who is focused on biblically sound relational traits. Traits which focus on the inside are selfish and hinder the building of intimacy. Men, when you focus your attention on your own interests and desires, you will reap a harvest of loneliness, guilt, anger, resentment, depression, physical pain, pity, and stress. And it's hard for any woman to be attracted to a man who is burdened with this kind of self-centered baggage.

Instead, set your focus on developing the traits which will encourage a deeper relationship with your mate. These traits are found in Galatians 5:22-23:

"Love, joy, peace, patience, kindness, goodness, faithfulness, gentleness and self-control" (NIV). These nine traits are words to grow by in developing intimacy. They reflect the character of Christ, and focusing on their development in our lives will show that we desire to be like Christ. What could be more attractive to a woman than a man who is becoming more like Christ in his attitudes and actions toward her? And what could better facilitate intimacy in a relationship than a man who is committed to expressing these nine service-oriented traits in his ministry to his wife?

Becoming a man of love, joy, peace, patience, kindness, goodness, faithfulness, gentleness, and self-control is a lifelong goal. These character traits don't happen automatically or instantaneously. They are the result of a process of growth in our lives which may involve many experiences. For example, I remember Emilie praying for more patience, and then realizing that patience comes from the experience of enduring tribulation. Be careful when you pray for the development of these traits in your life because each one comes about through changes in your life. But the rewards of intimacy in your marriage will be worth the change.

Men, if your married life isn't as rewarding as you would like, check your growth in these nine strategic traits. If you want the intimacy in your marriage to improve, begin to strengthen these ministry-oriented traits in your life. You will find that your wife will respond positively as she sees you becoming more Christlike.

Intimate Tips for Women

Emilie directs women to 1 Peter 3:1-6 when teaching them how to build intimacy in their marriages. She suggests that whether your husband is a believer or an unbeliever, he will respond favorably in the relationship if you follow these scriptural guidelines:

- 🐾 Be submissive to your husband; don't resist him or rebel against him.
- 🐾 Demonstrate your Christian faith through your life-style instead of preaching it.
- 🐾 Be loyal to your husband in every way, including sexually.
- 🐾 Take care to remain externally attractive.
- 🐾 Demonstrate the inner qualities of a quiet and gentle spirit.

Another principle a woman needs to keep in mind is never to attack her husband's ego. A man's outward display of ego strength is usually a cover-up for weaknesses and feelings of insecurity. If a woman attacks her man's ego she may drive him away from her instead of develop the intimacy she desires. He will be unable to perform sexually. He will lack sensitivity, understanding, and compassion. He will become withdrawn and noncommunicative, angry, and resentful. He may be easily tempted to infidelity by a woman who understands his ego needs.

Instead of attacking your husband, you should reverence him and lift him up. Men need to know that they are important to their wives and their children. A woman who is dedicated to supporting and encouraging her husband will find him eager to expand the horizons of their intimacy as a couple.

Is Intimacy Possible?

You may doubt that the level of intimacy we have

described in this chapter is possible in your marriage. Yes, it *is* possible! Just keep a few principles in mind.

First, both of you must be willing to submit yourselves to each other out of reverence for Christ according to Ephesians 5:21. That's the only way Emilie and I have been able to remain married for more than 33 years. Without mutual submission in every aspect of our lives, Satan would be able to enter in and destroy us with pride.

Second, intimacy is an attitude which grows into a blessing by biblical design—God's design. It doesn't just happen. It takes persistent prayer and discipline to apply God's principles to your marriage. May you be challenged to get into God's Word to see what He says about love, sex, and intimacy in married life.

Third, set goals and pursue them doggedly. Our definition of success is "progressive realization of worthwhile goals." Personally focus on the qualities which will make you a better husband or wife, and don't give up pursuing them. Identify the qualities which need extra attention and plan some activities which will help you make these qualities a part of your life.

Fourth, continue to love the Lord with all your heart. By actively loving God you plug yourself into the love which will foster intimacy in your marriage. Be a loving doer of the Word, and a doer in your marriage, instead of a passive listener or watcher.

Love, sex, and intimacy are ordained by God. He created them and pronounced them good. May each of you find, nurture, and enjoy the goodness God planned for the intimacy of your relationship.

9

Money Matters in a Great Marriage

> You must never think that you have made
> yourselves wealthy by your own power and
> strength. Remember that it is the Lord your
> God who has given you the power to become
> rich (Deut. 8:17-18, TEV).

Emilie and I began married life with $500 in the bank and an annual teacher's salary of $3,600, with take-home pay of $247 per month. We sat down at the dining room table on the first of each month and paid the bills, and sometimes there was too much month left at the end of our money. But neither of us came from wealthy families so we were content to begin at this level. Any money we had received while growing up was earned by hard work: Emilie in her mother's dress shop and I from paper routes and odd jobs around the neighborhood. We each brought to our marriage a solid work ethic and a responsible approach to saving and spending money.

Emilie and I have successfully continued our disciplines for handling money for more than 33 years. We have always agreed on our budgets and purchases. We have regularly given back to the Lord what He has so abundantly given us. We have maintained a disciplined savings habit. We have never lost control of our

credit. And we have established an investment program which includes life insurance, stocks, bonds,
real estate, etc. In this chapter we want to share with
you some fundamentals for money management we
have learned and practiced.

Good Money Management Is Imperative

For the Christian family, good money management
is imperative for at least three reasons. First, God
associates our ability to handle spiritual matters with
our ability to handle money. In Luke 16:11, Jesus
stated, "If you have not been trustworthy in handling
worldly wealth, who will trust you with true riches?"
(NIV). If we want to grow in spiritual responsibility
and blessing, we must prove our faithfulness in the
area of financial responsibility. God is not going to
trust us spiritually if we have been irresponsible with
our money.

Second, financial responsibility is important because we are only caretakers of what really belongs to
God. Psalm 24:1 declares, "The earth is the Lord's,
and all it contains" (NASB). You may *possess* many
things—home, car, furniture, boat, money—but you
don't *own* anything. Even your ability to earn money
comes from God (see Deut. 8:17-18). Everything belongs to Him. You are merely a steward of His property.
God holds you personally responsible to faithfully
manage for Him whatever money or possessions He
allows you to have.

Often we are tempted to grasp our possessions self-
ishly as if they belonged to us and not to God. I'll never
forget the beautiful blue 1972 Mercedes Benz I cher-
ished for about 10 years. I waxed it often to keep it
shining brightly, kept it in the garage when I wasn't
driving it, and dusted it every day.

Once when Emilie and I were away for a few days, our son Brad and a few buddies came home from college to go skiing. Brad saw my Mercedes in the garage and decided to take it to the mountains to impress his friends and any young ladies they might meet. He strapped the ski rack to the roof, loaded the skis and poles onto the rack, and headed for the slopes.

All went well until they started home. The ski rack vibrated loose and slid off, leaving a dent and a large scratch on the roof of my Mercedes. When I returned home, Brad broke the news. When I saw my damaged car I was mad at Brad for taking my car without asking, and devastated that he had allowed my prized car to be damaged. But it took me only a moment to regain my composure. God was using the incident to test my perspective on my car. "Gee, God, Your car has a scratch and a dent," I said. I drove God's Mercedes for another year and a half with the scratched and dented roof. Each time I looked at the damage it reminded me who really owned the car.

As caretakers of God's money and property we must obediently grow and nurture the spiritual fruit of self-control (see Galatians 5:22-23). Every couple we have counseled over the years regarding money problems had at least one member who lacked self-control. Money problems were just one of many undisciplined areas in their lives including maintenance of the home, yard, and automobile, spiritual life, personal hygiene, children, and on and on. These couples exemplify the "easy come, easy go" generation. They are irresponsible with their money and possessions and, consequently, always have problems in these areas. God wants to give to us abundantly, but He also wants us to exercise self-control over the management of what He gives.

Third, financial responsibility is necessary to help us avoid a number of major money mistakes. Most couples fall into one or more of the following traps because they have not appropriated biblically-based principles for the use of their money and possessions:

1. Getting into debt beyond your means to repay. We live in the now generation, and we don't like to save for something when we can buy it now on credit. But easily available credit can become a problem when we have no predetermined limits and guidelines for spending. I am not saying that you shouldn't go into debt. But undisciplined credit spending is a big mistake (see Romans 13:8).

2. Living a money-centered life. It is easy in our culture to get caught up in the pursuit of wealth and material possessions. But Scriptures like Matthew 6:19-24 and 1 Timothy 6:6-10 warn us that God is to be our focus, not money. Without careful, prayerful money management, we can be overly influenced by our money-centered society.

3. Trying to get rich quick. Once a reputable Christian man in our church urged me to buy some stock at $26 per share, promising me it could be sold at $40 per share within a month. I eagerly invested a large sum of money, only to lose it all when the "sure-fire" company went bankrupt. My overeagerness to make a financial killing cost us dearly. Proper money management will help you keep tantalizing schemes like these in perspective (see Prov. 28:22).

4. Withholding benevolence. According to Proverbs 11:24-25, if we give generously to God and others, we will receive everything we need. But we often turn that principle around by grabbing and holding onto everything we need and want, and giving only from the leftovers—if there are any. For the Christian, being a grabber instead of a giver is not only unscriptural, it is financially unprofitable.

5. *Using people.* When money becomes a priority in our lives, our relationships often suffer. We use people as stepping-stones to promotions or personal gain, or we see people as our customers instead of those we are to love, honor, and care for. We are in trouble when we scramble the saying "Love people and use things" to read "Use people and love things."

6. *Misplacing priorities.* When we overemphasize money in our lives, we try to beat God's system and do things our way. The order of the big three priorities in life—God, family, and work—often gets wrongly aligned to read:

> Work, family, God
> or work, God, family
> or family, work, God
> or family, God, work
> or God, work, family
> until we finally get it right:
> God, family, work.

At one point in my working experience I had to ask myself this very basic question: How much of my soul am I going to sell to my boss? Until I answered "no more," I was never satisfied because I was letting other people establish my priorities. When I took control of my life, I established the order of the big three in my life. Only when it was God first, family second, and work third was I really content in my job.

Principles for Financial Responsibility

Financial responsibility for Christian families can be categorized into three distinct actions concerning the resources God has entrusted to us: giving, receiving, and spending. When we discover God's principles for these three areas, and implement His principles with practical strategies, our needs will be met and our families blessed. Let's look closely at each area.[1]

Giving

Once I heard a comic on TV say, "I've been rich and I've been poor; and I like being rich better." For the Christian, the only reason to be rich is to have resources to carry on God's program. Does God need our wealth? No. Can God's purposes be carried out without our money? Yes! God doesn't need our possessions, but we do need to give. God doesn't care how much we give as deeply as He cares why we give. When we lovingly and obediently fulfill our role as givers—no matter what the amount—God will use what we give to minister to others and we will receive a blessing in return.

The Scriptures clearly show us many directions for our giving:

- ❧ To God through our tithes, gifts, and offerings (Prov. 3:9-10; 1 Cor. 16:2);
- ❧ To the poor (Prov. 19:17);
- ❧ To other believers in need (Rom. 12:13; Gal. 6:9-10);
- ❧ To those who minister to us (Gal. 6:6; 1 Tim. 5:17-18);
- ❧ To widows (1 Tim. 5:3-16);
- ❧ To family members (1 Tim. 5:8).

On the subject of giving to God, we have already determined that everything we have is His anyway. The question of how much we should actually give back to God in tithes, gifts, and offerings is debatable among Christians. Some insist on a literal tithe (10 percent) and others claim that grace allows each individual to give as he chooses. Without entering the debate, my point is simply that Christians are clearly instructed to return to the Owner of everything a portion of that which He has given to us. In this chapter I will use 10 percent to represent Christian giving, whether offered as a tithe or a freewill gift.

Second Corinthians 9:6-15 contains three excellent principles on the topic of giving. Read the passage for yourself and note the following principles:

Principle #1: We reap what we sow. If we sow sparingly we will reap sparingly. Plants cannot grow if no seeds have been planted. Cups cannot overflow unless water is continually poured into them. If you want an abundance, you must give an abundance. If you give little, you will reap little.

Principle #2: We are to be cheerful givers. We are not to give because we feel pressured to give, but freely and joyfully as in all other areas of ministry. We have attended a couple of churches which have helped worshipers grasp this truth. In the Mariner's Church in Newport Beach, California, no offering plates are passed. Church leaders believe that if God is working in your life, you will make the effort to place your gift in the mail slot in the wall. Another church we attended called the offering box in the foyer the "blessing box." Leaders in this church taught the principles of giving, then trusted parishioners to respond to God's Word instead of an offering plate. And whenever a special financial need arose, the elders brought it to the congregation and the need was met.

Principle #3: We will be blessed because of our obedience. The world will know we are obedient to God by our faithfulness in giving.

You may ask, "How can I give before I receive? Don't I need to have something before I can give it?" That may be the way we think, but that's not the way God thinks. Luke 6:39 states: "Give, and it will be given to you" (NIV). Only after we give are we ready to receive what God has for us.

Receiving

As giving Christians, we receive from several sources:

- ❧ From others giving to us (1 Cor. 9:11);
- ❧ From diligent work (Gen. 3:19; 1 Thess. 4:11-12; 2 Thess. 3:10-13);
- ❧ From creative endeavors (Prov. 31:13,24);
- ❧ From answers to prayer (Phil. 4:6; Jas. 4:2).

Emilie and I know a couple in Newport Beach who once suffered serious financial problems because the husband was having difficulty finding a job. About ten couples from their church banded together to cover their house payments, food, insurance premiums, car expenses, and household needs while the man was out of work. The couple had always been faithful givers; this was their opportunity to receive. Like them, you may be surprised at times to see how God provides for your needs through the giving of others.

A primary way we receive is in return for our own hard work. With all the government programs for the needy today, sometimes we are tempted to look for a handout instead of a job. But Paul clearly confronted that attitude when he wrote, "He who does not work shall not eat" (2 Thess. 3:10, TLB). Your diligence as a worker is an avenue by which God will bless you and meet your needs.

Like the Proverbs 31 woman, couples may sometimes receive supplementary income from their creative endeavors such as sewing, ironing, typing, woodworking, painting, or baking. Others may have the resources to open a business in their home such as selling and distributing cosmetics, cleaning supplies, kitchenware, or nutrition items. Maybe you also have a God-given talent that you can parlay into extra income.

James wrote: "The reason you don't have what you want is that you don't ask God for it" (Jas. 4:2, TLB). Since God owns everything we need, He is the ultimate source of everything we receive. We must ask Him to supply our needs, whether it's a certain salary, a refrigerator that costs $35, or a larger home. As we present our needs to Him, He may supply them through the giving of others, a temporary job or overtime, or a completely unknown source. But we must pray to Him and expect from Him because He is our source.

In Mark 10:29-30 Jesus teaches that if we leave houses, farms, and relatives for His sake, we will receive a hundred times as much as we give up. We have proved that this principle works. We have homes in Newport Beach, Laguna Beach, Santa Barbara, and Lake Arrowhead, and vacation homes in Scottsdale, Arizona; Chicago; and Stockbridge, Massachusetts. We have boats at the ocean and private jet planes. These assets didn't cost us one dime. They are at our disposal because they belong to Christian friends who give to us freely because somehow we have touched their lives along the way.

Spending

On the topic of spending, we first need to talk about *spendable income*. When you receive your paycheck, there is a very important number on it called *gross income*, the amount of money you earned before deductions. In order to figure your spendable income you need to deduct two standard expenses from your gross income.

First, you must deduct your giving to God—10 percent, for example. During a session at one of our seminars a man asked if giving should be figured on the gross or the net. A pastor in the group retorted, "Do you want to get blessed on the gross or the net?" Good point. If you are giving a percentage of your true earnings, you must figure your giving on gross income. When you consider your giving a standard expense which is taken off the top of your earnings, you will be more faithful than if you consider it an option.

Second, you must deduct local, state, and federal income taxes, approximately 17 percent, including social security. (Other deductions from gross income such as medical, dental, or life insurance premiums, credit union payments, payroll savings, retirement contributions, or annuities, etc. are figured elsewhere in your spending.) These two deductions equal approximately 27 percent, and the 73 percent which remains we call *spendable income*. Your spendable income is the amount you have the most control over.

Some Christian financial advisors suggest that spendable income be allocated according to the 10-70-20 plan. According to this plan, 10 percent of your spendable income should be reserved for savings and investments, including any deductions from your paycheck for these purposes.

General living expenses should be confined to 70 percent of your spendable income. This category includes all of the following:

Housing. Housing consists of all expenses necessary to operate the home including mortgage/rent, property taxes, insurance, maintenance, and utilities. When budgeting utilities, be sure to average your payments over a 12-month period.

Food. Include all groceries, paper goods, and non-food products normally purchased at a grocery store. Include items like bread and milk which are often purchased in between regular shopping trips. Do not include lunches or dinners at restaurants, which is another category. If you do not know your actual food expenses, keep a detailed spending record for 30-45 days.

Transportation. In this category you have car payments, auto insurance, gas and oil, licenses, maintenance, etc. Another transportation expense is for depreciation, setting aside money to repair and/or replace your automobile. The minimum amount set aside should be enough to keep the car in decent repair, and then to replace it every four or five years. If replacement funds are not available in the budget, the minimum amount set aside should cover maintenance costs.

Annual or semi-annual auto insurance premiums should be set aside monthly to avoid the crisis of a neglected expense. If you ride a bus or train to work, fares should be budgeted in this category.

Insurance. Include health, life, and disability not categorized under housing or transportation. Also include amounts deducted from your paycheck for these items.

Entertainment and recreation. Include vacations, camping trips, dining out, club dues, sporting equipment, hobby expenses, and athletic events. Don't forget little league and booster club expenses, etc. The only effective method to budget for entertainment and recreation is to decide on a reasonable amount for your family and stay within it.

Clothing. Determine your monthly budget in this area by dividing a year's worth of expenditures by 12. The minimum amount should be $10 per family member per month.

Medical. Include insurance deductibles, doctor bills, eyeglasses, prescriptions and over-the-counter medicines, orthodontia, etc.

Miscellaneous. This category is a general catchall for items like child-care expenses for working mothers, private education costs, allowances, laundry expenses, gifts, etc.

The final 20 percent of your spendable income should be earmarked for payment of debts (loans, notes, credit cards, etc.) and emergencies. Sometimes called a buffer or margin, this amount consists of any money left over after expenses. Most couples with financial difficulty will not have any money in this account. Those who include a margin account in their budgets will find it to be a helpful fund for special projects, offerings, gifts, additional savings, or future education expenses.

For every $1,000 earned per month, your 10-70-20 figures would look like this:

Total income	$ 1,000
Less giving	(100)
Less taxes	(170)
Total spendable income	$ 730
10% savings and investments	(73)
70% living expenses	(511)
20% debts or buffer	(146)

Financial Freedom

The goal of financial responsibility is financial freedom. In order to be financially free you must meet these qualifications:

1. Your income exceeds your expenses;
2. You are able to pay your debts as they fall due;
3. You have no unpaid bills;
4. And, above all, you are *content* at your present income level.

If we intend to honor God with our giving, we must also honor Him with our responsible stewardship of the remaining nine-tenths of our income.

Use the Monthly Income and Expenses worksheet at the end of this chapter to evaluate your present spending habits. If your expenses are higher than your income, you can use the worksheet to identify areas where you can cut costs. You may want to consult a financial advisor for assistance.

Why Families Suffer Financially

Most of the experts in family financial counseling list three main faults which lead to financial tragedy:

1. Failure to budget income and expenses. Instead of telling their money where to go, many couples are always wondering where their money went. They don't chart their income and plan their expenses accordingly; they just spend what comes in—and then some.

Handling family finances must be disciplined by planning income and expenses. It's the difference between spending on purpose and by accident. Discipline in finances means you cannot always go out to dinner on the spur of the moment when your entertainment budget is low. Both partners need to be in on long-range budget planning and then help each other hold to the decisions made together. Having long-range financial goals will help you make short-range financial decisions.

2. Failure to plan for emergencies. Unanticipated financial emergencies consist of expenses which generally are not included in the monthly budget. They are expenses like birthday, wedding, and Christmas gifts; home, appliance, or auto repairs or replacement; vacation expenses; insurance premiums; and education expenses. Since they are not predictable expenses, we usually don't plan for them and they are a financial burden when they occur.

Emilie and I have a special emergency savings account to cover such items. Each month I write a check to this account, and we allow it to build up untouched. When an unexpected expense arrives, we transfer the needed amount from the emergency account into the checking account and pay the bill. This special fund has reduced a great deal of stress in our family. Emilie looks at me and says, "Bob, you're so smart!" My face lights up with a big smile because my leadership has been noticed and appreciated.

Misuse of credit. Banks and lending institutions are eager to let us use their money. Most of us have received occasional notices in the mail informing us that we have "qualified" for a $5,000 line of credit. Credit cards are available for a signature and sometimes sent to our homes without request. I hear some people say, "If the banks are dumb enough to send me their money, I'll take it." And that's just what the lending companies want: eager and irresponsible borrowers.

I follow a ritual in responding to unsolicited credit cards and offers of lines of credit. I hold them in my left hand, then take a pair of scissors in my right hand and cut them up. I don't want their money because it is too easy to become a slave to credit. We have found that we would rather do without than be obligated to repayment.

Some Christian counselors suggest that we should live on a cash basis only—no credit whatsoever. For those who are in serious financial trouble, I agree that cutting up credit cards may be the best solution. But I also believe credit cards have their proper place in a family's financial plan. They provide good records for spending, they are safer to carry than cash, and they help a family develop a good credit record. But credit cards also have their shortcomings: very high interest rates, service charges, and late payment fees. Furthermore, credit card users tend to buy more than they can afford.

If families are to use credit cards they must be mature in their financial management. Our family has only charged items which we can pay off when the statement arrives. We have rarely used our credit cards for installment purchases. The cost of credit card money is too great.

Gaining Financial Maturity

Our seminar ministry to the Body of Christ focuses on time management and home organization. Consequently Emilie and I are always thinking about how individuals and families can be more efficient in their use of time and money. We have found that the overall goal of financial maturity is achieved by taking many smaller thoughtful steps concerning income and expenses. Here are several of the helpful steps we have practiced:

❧ Consider God's Word as the final authority on your financial matters.

❧ Realize that God owns everything, and He gives to us as we demonstrate responsibility and trustworthiness with His resources.

❧ Remove all personal debts which do not fit into your budget. Apply for a bill consolidation loan if necessary.

❧ Develop sales resistance. Plan a budget within the limits of your financial goals, then say no to any expenditure which does not fit within it.

❧ Concentrate on meeting your material needs before gratifying your wants.

❧ Look for the best buys on items by shopping around before purchasing. Consider buying good used items instead of new items by scouring the classified ads and secondhand stores.

❧ Give God the opportunity to provide your material needs. Make your requests known to Him in prayer, and ask others to pray with you about your needs.

❧ Become a do-it-yourself person. Instead of buying an item, consider borrowing or buying how-to books which will help you make the item at a lower cost.

❧ Look for ways to increase your income by using your creative skills and spare time.

❧ If you cannot use a credit card responsibly, cut it up or send it back and use cash for your purchases.

❧ If you cannot dig yourself out of a financial hole, seek the help of qualified others (see Prov. 11:14). Many churches have staff members who can assist you in this area. Consider also professional counselors and local agencies which offer help in this area. Check with the Better Business Bureau for referrals.

❧ Help your children learn financial responsibility by teaching them at a young age the proper use of money.

May each of us, with God's help, be good stewards of all His riches. May God say to us as He did to the servant in Matthew 25:21: "Well done, good and faithful slave; you were faithful with a few things, I will put you in charge of many things; enter into the joy of your master" (NASB).

WORKSHEET: Monthly Income and Expenses

INCOME

Gross Income (monthly)
    Salary   _____
    Interest   _____
    Dividends   _____
    Notes   _____
    Rents   _____
    Other   _____

    Total gross income   _____

Standard Expenses
    Giving to God (10%)   _____
    Income taxes (17%)   _____

    Total standard expenses   _____

Spendable Income
(gross income less standard expenses) _____

EXPENSES

Savings and Investments (10%)
Savings _____
Investments _____

Total savings and investments _____

Living Expenses (70%)
Housing
  Mortgage/rent _____
  Insurance _____
  Property taxes _____
  Electricity _____
  Gas _____
  Water _____
  Sanitation _____
  Telephone _____
  Maintenance _____
  Other _____

  Total housing _____
Food _____
Transportation
  Payments _____
  Gas/oil _____
  Insurance _____
  Licenses _____
  Taxes _____
  Maintenance _____
  Other _____

  Total transportation _____

Insurance
    Life   _____
    Medical   _____
    Other   _____

    Total insurance   _____

Entertainment and Recreation
    Eating out   _____
    Amusements   _____
    Baby-sitters   _____
    Vacation   _____

    Total entertainment and
    recreation   _____

Clothing   _____

Medical
    Doctors   _____
    Dentists   _____
    Prescriptions   _____
    Other   _____

    Total medical   _____

Miscellaneous
    Toiletries/cosmetics   _____
    Beauty/hair care   _____
    Laundry/cleaning   _____
    Allowances/lunches   _____
    Subscriptions   _____
    Gifts (incl. Christmas)   _____
    Education   _____
    Other   _____
    Total miscellaneous   _____

Total living expenses   _____

Debts and Emergencies (20%)
    Credit card payments   ———————

                                        ———————

                                        ———————

                                        ———————

    Loan and note payments ———————
    Emergencies   ———————
    Other   ———————

    Total debts and emergencies   ———————

INCOME VERSUS EXPENSES

Total spendable income   ———————

Total expenses (10-70-20)   ———————

Monthly bottom line (income less
        expenses)

                            ———————

If income exceeds expenses, where will you direct your surplus income?

If expenses exceed income, where will you increase income or cut expenses?

10

Growing as Great Parents

Train up a child in the way he should go,
even when he is old he will not depart from
it (Prov. 22:6, NASB)

Our first three years of marriage were spent in
a cozy paradise for two. Emilie and I did what we
wanted when we wanted—trips to the beach, picnics
in the park, spending money on ourselves. Then we
decided to start having children. As Emilie's first
due date approached we excitedly thought about and
planned for our coming child—her name, her bedroom, her colors, her clothes. Our conversations began
to center around the pronoun *her* instead of *us*.

One morning Emilie went to the doctor for her
routine examination. "Are you ready to have a baby?"
he asked after the exam. Emilie called me at school
and asked me the same question. We were a little
uncertain about this new adventure, but we were
ready. All of our anticipation came to a head that
evening as Jenny was born. She had finally arrived,
the one we had so wanted and prayed for. Flashbulbs
flashed, flowers and cards arrived at the hospital,
phone calls were placed to close friends and relatives.
After three days in the hospital Emilie was able to
bring our baby home.

When Jenny came through the door our life-style changed drastically. Where we had been living for ourselves, we suddenly realized we had to include one other person in our family circle. Where we were once free to come and go as we pleased, we were forced to develop a schedule built around our little girl. A new and far-reaching identity had been added to our relationship as a couple. We were now parents.

Our most pressing question was, "How do we raise this new gift from God?" Lots of people on the sidelines were giving advice. Dr. Benjamin Spock had a good book on children's illnesses which we used to diagnose a cold, measles, chicken pox, fever, etc. But his philosophy of raising children was too liberal. And in those days there were no Christian books, tapes, radio programs, videos, or MOPs (Mothers of Preschoolers) groups available to parents. How were we to become equipped for our new role?

Instead of relying on outside help, we relied on the Bible and what it told us about children and how to raise them. We talked to other Christian parents whom we respected. We talked to both our mothers. And we prayed a lot. Our one practical goal was to raise godly children who learned to take on as much responsibility as they were capable of handling. We wanted to equip them to someday obey Genesis 2:24-25 by leaving our home in order to begin successful homes of their own. In this chapter we want to share some of the principles we learned and practiced along the way which helped us reach our goal.

The Discipline of Training

Our key verse for this chapter challenges us to "train up" our children. The word train has a special emphasis beyond mere talking or pleading with our children. Training is a commitment to the individual being trained which persists through the victories and defeats of the process. We use Deuteronomy 6:7 as a basic guideline: "And you shall teach them [God's commandments] diligently to your sons and shall talk of them when you sit in your house and when you walk by the way and when you lie down and when you rise up" (NASB). Training is a 24-hours-a-day, seven-days-a-week process. We are to use every life situation, wherever and whenever it happens, to train our children.

Here are three important principles which form a frame of reference for the important ministry of training your children:

1. The influence of the parents far outweighs any other influence in your child's life. Don't ever feel that you aren't important in the training of your child because you are "only" a parent instead of a teacher, pastor, or coach. The home holds the upper hand in determining how happy, secure, and stable a child will be. What happens in your home makes a greater impact on your child than any outside influence. This means your home life must be conducted with a purpose, a smile, an affirming touch, and an encouraging word.

According to a recent study by the California Congress of Parents, Teachers, and Students, Inc., parental training and involvement has more influence on a child's success in school than the school, the quality of his teachers, or the amount of money spent on his education. Children achieve more readily when their parents read to them, value and transmit their cultural heritage to them, when families do things together, and when parents value their children's academic success.

We were visiting some friends in San Diego recently and, as we were finishing dinner, their four-year-old daughter Heather asked her daddy, "Daddy, what is the best thing that happened to you today?" Heather's daddy is a police officer and he works in such a negative environment that his family realized they needed to deliberately speak positively. Heather's daddy answered the question, and then she went around the table asking each of us the same question. Emilie and I were impressed that our friends were building into their children uplifting experiences like Heather's question. As parents we are to uplift our children.

2. Knowing the differences in your children's temperaments helps explain some of the difficulties in training them. Some children are more naturally lovable or easier to handle than others. How you relate to these differences greatly determines how your child will turn out. And some parents are more prone to nurturing than others. A nurturing parent will have an easier time training children than a non-nurturing parent. The best combination for parenting is a nurturing parent with an easy child; the most difficult combination is a non-nurturing parent with a difficult child. Being aware of the differences in temperament in yourself and your children will help you better understand how to train them.

3. The relationship between a father and mother is critical in determining the success of a child's development. Our first job as parents is to be the best husband and wife we can be. When children see a good relationship between Mom and Dad they are well on their way to being emotionally balanced. If you want to have loving children, you must be a loving couple. If there is disharmony between the two of you the children will sense it and develop insecurities at a young age.

Healthy parents with a good marriage relationship produce healthy children with a good child-to-parent relationship.

When they were children, Jenny and Brad would come to us quite often wanting to be assured that Emilie and I loved each other. When we gave them that assurance they experienced real peace of mind. We are convinced that the stronger and healthier our bond is as husband and wife, the fewer problems we will have as parents.

If anyone must take the lead in this process it must be the husband/father. In his book, *How to Really Love Your Child*, Dr. Ross Campbell states: "The husband who will take full, total, and overall responsibility for his family, and take the initiative in conveying his love to his wife and children will experience unbelievable rewards: a loving, appreciative, helping wife who will be her loveliest for him; children who are safe, secure, content and able to grow to be their best. I personally have never seen marriages fail if these priorities are met. Every failing marriage I have seen has somehow missed these priorities. Fathers, the initiative must be ours."[1]

Love Them Unconditionally

We hear the term "unconditional love" quite often in the Christian community. It means "I love you no matter what you do." Unconditional love reflects the selfless *agape* love which God has displayed toward us. Unconditional love is contrasted with conditional love which says, "I love you only if you do what pleases me." As parents we must love our children unconditionally, not based on what they do or don't do but on who they are—the children God gave us. We may not always like our children's behavior, but we can always love them.

Emilie and I remember when our children were in junior high school, and the popular hair length for Brad and style of dress for Jenny were different than what we preferred. Brad let his hair get longer and Jenny's style of dress was more casual than cute, but we decided to love them anyway. We didn't let length of hair or style of dress separate us from our children. We continued to love them through this transition period of their lives. And we are so glad we took this tack, because today Brad is immaculate in his dress. He works for a computer firm with a very strict dress code, and he always looks like he stepped right out of *GQ* Magazine. Jenny is a good example of how to dress with thrifty class. She is an expert at putting together attractive outfits from items purchased at bargain prices.

Only when we love our children unconditionally can we prevent problems in their lives arising from guilt, insecurity, fear, and feelings of low self-esteem. If our love is conditional our children will never be able to match our expectations. Insecurity, anxiety, and low self-esteem will haunt them as they grow into adulthood. But when we love them unconditionally, our children begin to feel good about themselves and grow to genuinely like themselves. With these positive attitudes they will be more able to relax and control their fears and anxieties.

Children are always asking parents, "Do you love me?" The way you answer them will contribute greatly to their development. A child's behavior will reflect how he perceives your answer to this question. If he feels that you love him, he will usually behave properly. If he feels you don't love him, he will often try to gain your attention through negative behavior.

Children are always checking our verbal and non-verbal reactions to their antics to see if we really love them. Your teenagers will bring home startling news just to see how you handle the information. We recommend that you stay "cool," and don't hear or see everything.

Parents can nourish self-esteem in their children by letting them know that they are special, recognizing each child as an individual and avoiding comparisons between children. Concentrate on recognizing your child's efforts, not just his accomplishments. We found that immediate praise gave us the behavior we sought in our children. On the other hand, when their behavior was not what we wanted, we took equal time to discipline them. We found that when our children began to act up they were telling us, "Mom and Dad, I don't feel loved." Emilie and I would treat their misbehavior as a signal that their needs for love were not being fully met.

Many of the problems with today's children—bad attitudes, disrespect for authority, emotional instability, drugs, crime—exist because our children do not feel genuinely loved, accepted, and cared for. Oh, we love them all right, but we haven't been able to transmit that love to them. That's because parents don't have a proper perspective on how to relate to their children. Unconditional love and respect for each other is so important. We must love and respect our children, even when their actions are different from what we want or expect.

You may be able to provide a loving influence for your children in your home, but what about the time your child spends under the influence and control of others—teachers, neighbors, peers, and even strangers? We prayed continually for God to bring good teachers, coaches, and friends into our children's lives. He answered those prayers by providing some wonderful role models for Jenny and Brad. Love your children unconditionally while they are with you, and trust God to bring others into their lives who will love them also.

Focused Attention

Ever since our children were very young both Emilie and I were present and involved in their activities at home, school, church, and community. During their formative years our life as parents was our children. When Brad played in a ball game, we were in the bleachers. When Jenny tried out for cheerleader, we were there to the end. For five straight years during their high school years, we attended every game Brad played and every event Jenny cheered for—whether home or away. Sometimes it was raining so hard we couldn't see the playing field. Sometimes the gym was so hot Emilie and I both sweated away five pounds. But whenever and wherever they were involved, we were there.

Did we always like being there? No! Did it cost us something to be there? Yes! Then why did we do it? Because we wanted to display our love for them through our focused attention on them and their interests. For us it was sports and athletics; for you it might be theatre, orchestra, or art. Your focused attention through your physical presence and participation will make your child feel like he is the most important person in the world.

Another way we displayed focused attention on our children was through our "memory plate." Through the years we have kept a plate in the cupboard with the words "An Occasion to Remember" inscribed on it. Whenever a family member had a special occasion—birthday, good grades, promotion, award, etc.—we would honor the individual by serving his or her meal on the memory plate. And whenever one of the children had a disappointing day, such as not making the varsity baseball team, the memory plate was used as a way to lift up drooping spirits. We endeavored always to honor each other in our family, but the memory plate was a very special, focused honor.

A significant expression of focused attention on Jenny came when she approached her 16th birthday. Our family had agreed that Jenny would not be eligible to officially accept a date until she was 16, and that first date would be with Dad. What a great time I had planning this grand event. I wanted her to experience how a young lady should be treated on a date. I gave her a proper invitation, presented her with a corsage, opened the doors for her, and seated her at the dinner table of a nice restaurant. We had a wonderful, open conversation that evening about boys and dating which Jenny still talks about. I know she will want Craig to be their daughter Christine's first date too.

One of the family activities that really worked for us was our "family conference." We started out meeting for family conference at breakfast before church on Sunday mornings. When the children reached the fifth and sixth grades we moved the meeting to Friday evenings. When their evenings began filling up with high school activities, we moved the meeting back to Sunday morning.

We used this time to key in on important topics brought up by Emilie, Jenny, Brad, or me. We knew that if the children were part of the decision-making process they would be more likely to share the responsibility for the decision. If there were no particular topics to be discussed, we used the family conference for friendly conversation. This meeting was such a high priority for us that we blocked out the time on the calendar. We did not allow anything to interfere with this focused family time.[2]

Yes, focused attention on your children will take lots of time. Time is one of our most precious commodities. We don't have enough time to fulfill all our obligations. We must be very selective in the kinds of activities we undertake. And chief among our investments should be time spent with our children.

I talked to a father recently who told me he quit his job because his boss insisted that he work 12 hours a day for six days a week. He said no to his boss and his job because he wanted to spend more time with his family than his job allowed. He paid a high price for his decision, but I'm sure God will honor his decision by leading him to another job with hours which are more conducive to family life.

If you need help in budgeting your time for better family life, I recommend the first several chapters in Emilie's book *Survival for Busy Women*. These chapters will help you set goals and determine priorities for your time.

Staying in Touch

When we were raising our children there was practically no media exposure on child abuse or homosexuality. Today we are so bombarded with the reality of these problems that many moms and dads shy away from physical contact with their children, fearing they will encourage sexual disorientation. Yet research shows that children who are lovingly touched and hugged by their parents experience normal sexual development. As a classroom teacher I found that I got along great with my students when I transmitted my acceptance to them through a hug, an arm around the shoulder, or a pat on the head. Coaches use this technique with great success in their athletic programs. Parents who love their children with physical contact are excellent role models for healthy boys and girls.

Emilie and I found that our style of physical contact varied as each child grew older. For example, when Brad was in junior high school he announced to us that he didn't want us to kiss him in front of his friends anymore. We honored his request, but we would sneak into his room at night and kiss him while he slept.

The father plays a large part in developing proper sexual identification in his children when he meets their emotional needs for physical contact. Girls need their fathers' help in developing their self-image and sexual identity. I remember how Jenny would reach out for my approval by asking if I thought she was cute, if her dress fit properly, or if her hair looked right. The father's effectiveness in meeting his daughter's emotional needs will help her formulate these two key qualities. A father helps his daughter develop self-approval by demonstrating with his hugs that he approves of her. If a father withholds his approval and physical affection, she will find someone else—perhaps someone her parents would not approve—who will meet her need.

Boys seem to call out for physical contact at an earlier age than girls. However, a girl's need for contact seems to peak at around 11 or 12 years of age. Boys start out needing more attention to their emotional needs at an early age, but their need seems to decrease as they get older. Girls don't need as much attention at the outset, but their needs increase as they approach adolescence. This has significant implications for parents. I remember when Jenny, as a young lady who was already married, said "Dad, you don't hug me as much as you used to." What an eye-opener for me! I thought she would need less physical contact from me, but she was telling me she needed more. Dad, meet your daughter's emotional needs by giving her special attention through your hugs and kisses.

Seeing Eye-to-Eye

Another important element of our parenting practice has been eye contact. Our eyes are a primary means by which we can express our love for our children. We must be careful not to love them through eye contact only when they meet our conditional standards, but to love them unconditionally with our loving looks. Dr. Ross Campbell states, "The more parents make eye contact with their children as a means of expressing their love, the more the child is nourished with love and the fuller his emotional tank."[3]

As an elementary school teacher I was drawn to those students who could look me in the eye when they talked to me. They were usually the most popular students in class too. When children cannot look adults in the eye it indicates that their emotional needs are not being met. When Brad or Jenny were young, we would take their faces into our hands and ask them to look into our eyes when we wanted to talk to them. When they wouldn't look us in the eye we knew there was some grievance of the heart or spirit. At that point Emilie and I moved into action to correct whatever was preventing their willingness to meet us eye to eye.

If we only use eye contact with our children in a negative way, as when we are disciplining them, the child will treat eye contact as a negative experience with parents. Some parents stare their young children down in order to bring about the proper behavior.

But when the child gets older he may only associate eye-to-eye contact with anger, depression, resentment, or insecurity. We must be careful to use eye contact for giving positive emotional communication.

Filling their Emotional Tanks

Many experts on child development talk about a child's "emotional tank." There was no such term around when we were raising children or when I was teaching school. Dr. Ross Campbell shares:

> Parents need to understand that each child has an emotional tank. Each child has certain emotional needs, and whether these emotional needs are met (through love, understanding, discipline, etc.) determines many things:

- How a child feels; whether he is content, angry depressed, or joyful.
- It affects his behavior; whether he is obedient, whiny, perky, playful, or withdrawn.

> The fuller the tank the more positive the feelings and the better the behavior.... Only if the emotional tank is full, can a child be expected to be at his best or to do his best.[4]

When a child's emotional tank is full he will behave well, earn good grades, and like himself and others. The child whose emotional tank is low or empty will have a poor chance for success. He will cause discipline problems, his self-esteem will be low, his grades will be low or failing, and he won't like or trust others.

Your Child's Emotional Tank

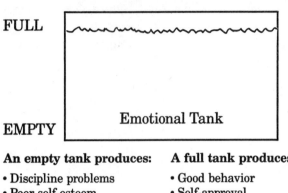

FULL

Emotional Tank

EMPTY

An empty tank produces:	**A full tank produces:**
• Discipline problems	• Good behavior
• Poor self-esteem	• Self-approval
• Failing grades	• Good grades
• Dislike for others	• Acceptance of others
• Distrust of others	• Eye contact

A child's behavior will tell you how full his emotional tank is. If your child's tank is low, he needs more attention, eye contact, and physical contact from you. Some good friends of ours recently invested $30,000 in a chemical dependency rehabilitation program for their 16-year-old daughter. A daily contribution to her emotional tank during her childhood would have been far less costly for all concerned.

Help Them Leave

A primary role of parents today is to equip their children to leave the home during young adulthood to begin homes and families of their own. One of the tragedies we see in relationships today is that some husbands and wives have not left their parents' homes. According to Genesis 2:24, men (and women too) are to leave their fathers and mothers in order to marry and form a new family. We must raise our children to leave our homes.

A few years ago we heard a letter read on Dr. James Dobson's program, "Focus on the Family," which a mother had written to her son in order to formally break his attachment to his parents' home. Perhaps reading this letter will help you prepare to cut the apron strings with your children:

Dear Paul,

This is the most important letter I have ever written to you, and I hope you will take it as seriously as I intend it. I have given a great amount of thought and prayer to the matter I want to convey, and I believe I am right in what I've intended to do.

For the past several years, you and I have been involved in a painful tug-of-war. You have been struggling to free yourself of my values and my wishes for your life. At the same time, I have been trying to hold you to what we both know is right. Even at the risk of nagging, I have been saying, "Go to church," "Choose the right friends," "Make good grades in school," "Live a Christian life," "Prepare wisely for your future," etc. I'm sure you've gotten tired of this urging and warning, but I have only wanted the best for you. This is the only way I knew to keep you from making some of the mistakes so many others have made.

However, I've thought all of this over during the last month and I believe that my job as your mother is now finished. Since the day you were born, I have done my best to do what was right for you. I have not always been successful—I've made mistakes and I've failed in many ways. Someday you will learn how difficult it is to be a good parent, and perhaps then you'll understand me better than you do now. But there's one area where I have never wavered. I've loved you with everything that is within me. It is impossible to convey the depth of my love for you through the years, and that affection is as great today as it's ever been. It will continue to be there in the future, although our relationship will change from this moment. As of now, you are free. You may reject God or accept Him, as you choose. Ultimately, you will answer only to Him anyway. You may marry whomever you wish without protest from me. You may go to UCLA or USC or any other college of your selection. You may fail or succeed in each of life's responsibilities. *The umbilical cord is now broken.*

I am not saying these things out of bitterness or anger. I still care what happens to you and am concerned for your welfare. I will pray for you daily and if you come to me for advice, I'll offer my opinion. But the responsibility now shifts from my shoulders to yours. You are a man now, and you're entitled to make your own decisions—regardless of the consequences. Throughout your life I've tried to build a foundation of values which would prepare you for this moment of manhood and independence. That time has come, and my record is in the books.

I have confidence in you, son. You are gifted and have been blessed in so many ways. I believe God will lead you and guide your footsteps, and I am optimistic about the future. Regardless of the outcome, I will always have a special tenderness in my heart for my beloved son.

Sincerely,

Your Mother

The concept in this letter has really helped us formulate what we do today in order for us to reach our long-range goal of setting our children free.

Don't Believe the Lie

One of the tragedies of the Christian family is that we often believe Satan's lie that parents can be over-committed in their schedules and still meet the emotional needs of their children. We have been brainwashed into thinking that a better house is more important than better children. Emilie and I meet many women at our seminars who are more interested in being better organized than in being better mothers. The following letter is a good example of this attitude:

> Dear Emilie:
>
> I've been so busy with my full time teaching job that I don't know where to turn. It is really difficult to get everything done that I would like to do, especially the nights when I get home so exhausted I can barely get dinner on the table. Any suggestions? I know you have them, it just seems that your ideas are more geared to the woman who is at home with more time to do all these things. I just never seem to catch my breath long enough. I hope you can give me some additional suggestions for beating the fatigue that goes along with this kind of schedule.
>
> I enjoy my job, but sometimes I'm overwhelmed with everything else I have to do. I especially do not enjoy spending the weekend playing catch-up with the cleaning and

the yard work. I've read your books over and over, and I try to follow the suggestions. But some days I'm so tired I start to fall behind. Help!

I ask God for His strength to get me through the difficult days and I would appreciate it if you would remember me in your prayers also.

Thanks so much for being my friend.

Love,

Kathy

This woman believes Satan's lie; she's too busy! My advice to her is to quit work. I know these are difficult words in our present cultural climate. But no money is worth the stress, pain, or frustration she is facing in her hectic life-style. Yes, we can give her some basic suggestions for coping with her schedule. But God never intended for His creatures to endure such frustration.

And Kathy is no rare exception. There are thousands of women (and men) who could have written this letter. I challenge all of us as parents to evaluate our priorities. We can only juggle so many balls at one time. When the balls begin to fall around us, it's time to eliminate some of them. May God direct you in the very important decisions you must make to assure that your children's emotional needs are being met.

11

Shaping Great Children through Discipline

Fathers, do not provoke your children to anger; but bring them up in the discipline and instruction of the Lord" (Eph. 6:4, NASB).

One topic that all parents are concerned about is discipline. It seems that as a society we have not made much progress in this area. As new parents 30 years ago, Emilie and I had the same questions about discipline which abound today. All parents want good, obedient children, but we're not exactly sure how to accomplish this end.

As young Christian parents, Emilie and I wanted to understand and apply scriptural principles for discipline. We relied on certain verses of Scripture on the subject which were old standbys:

- "He who spares his rod hates his son, but he who loves him disciplines him diligently" (Prov. 13:24, NASB).
- "Discipline your son while there is hope, and do not desire his death" (Prov. 19:18, NASB).
- "Train up a child in the way he should go, even when he is old he will not depart from it" (Prov. 22:6, NASB).

> ❧ "Do not hold back discipline from the child, although you beat him with the rod, he will not die" (Prov. 23:13, NASB).
>
> ❧ "The rod and reproof give wisdom, but a child who gets his own way brings shame to his mother" (Prov. 29:15, NASB).
>
> ❧ "Fathers, do not exasperate your children, that they may not lose heart" (Col. 3:21, NASB).

As we endeavored to follow these guidelines, we discovered a great motivator for disciplining our children: *Rewarding good behavior is better than punishing poor behavior.* Whenever our children did something good we would praise them, praise them, praise them. We continue this principle with our grandchildren. In our kitchen drawer we have a stack of cute bear stickers which read, "I was caught being good." When the grandchildren are over for a visit and we see one of them doing something good, we make a big deal out of it. Emilie will yell out, "I caught Bevan picking up his toys!" We apply one of the bear stickers to his T-shirt and he is so proud. Of course the other children also want stickers, so they are encouraged to get "caught" being good. We have learned that positive reinforcement fills a child's emotional tank. And the fuller his tank, the better the child will respond to training.

As we learned to accentuate the child's positives, we also learned the value of eliminating our negatives by saying "I'm sorry" to our children when we blew it. If you don't apologize when you wrong your children, you will cause anger and resentment between them which will short-circuit their training. Learn to apply 1 John 1:9 to these situations and then move on with the positive training of your children.

Balancing Training and Punishment

From our understanding of Scriptures we knew that God was a God of love *and* of discipline. Emilie and I wanted to transmit love to our children through positive reinforcement before punishing them through discipline. We also knew that discipline is not only a matter of punishment, but also of training. Training is the discipline of teaching our children to do right; punishment is the discipline of correcting our children for doing wrong. One of our goals for our young children was to focus on the discipline of training. We wanted Jenny and Brad to become self-controlled, independent, and valuable members of society.

When our children were growing up we actively practiced the principles of training found in Deuteronomy 6:6-7. We taught values at every opportunity. We trained our children using every type of communication available. We guided them by example, provided learning experiences which were fun, provoked discussions around television programs, and devised other creative training experiences for them.

We found with our children that the better trained they were, the less punishment they needed. Our early emphasis on training led to well-disciplined children who needed a minimum of punishment. Many parents err by being too casual with training when the children are young, resulting in discipline problems as the children get older.

As illustrated on the chart on the following page, parents who provide strong training during the early stages of a child's growth spend less time on punishment when the child gets older. But the parent who is lax on training when the child is young will spend a lot of time and energy punishing the child as he gets older. We see misbehaving children in shopping

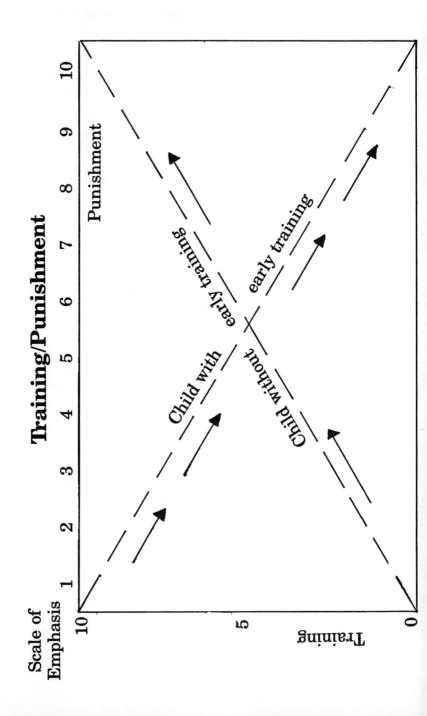

Training/Punishment

Scale of
Emphasis

Punishment

Child with early training

early training

Child without early training

Training

10

5

0

1 2 3 4 5 6 7 8 9 10

malls, markets, churches, and schools and know that they are the products of little training in the home. We urge parents all the time, "Don't let your four-year-old control your home." At one conference on parenting we attended, a parent asked the speaker, "What do you do when your four-year-old won't put on her dress?" With little hesitation he replied, "You stuff her into it." In some cases of early training, that's what it takes.

How a child responds to discipline depends primarily on how much he feels loved and accepted. As the two lists below suggest, training children with love produces a much more positive response than punishment without love:

Training with Love Produces...	Punishment without Love Produces...
Love	Anger
Compassion	Hatred
Sensitivity	Resentment
Understanding	Defiance
Forgiveness	Resentment
Nurturing	Rebellious
Guidance	Self-centered
Kindness	Obstinacy
Affection	Coldness
Giving	Taking
Obedience	Resistance

The "Board of Education"

As much as we wanted to focus on the positive training of our two special, God-given blessings, there were times when we needed to apply the "board of education" through punishment. When these times came along Emilie and I wanted to discipline them in such a way that showed them our love without provoking them to anger (see Eph. 6:4). Through the years we developed five guidelines for the discipline of punishment. Practicing them with our children seemed to answer our concerns both for loving our children and not provoking them to anger.

First, we only punished them for defiant behavior or when a well-understood rule was broken.

Second, we reviewed with the child why he was being punished. We would ask the question, "Do you understand why you are being punished?" We continued to discuss the issue until they understood the "why."

Third, from the time our children were four years old we spanked them with a paddle on the rear end. We were very firm with three or four swats until they cried. Over the years we had to exercise this form of punishment only a few times.

Fourth, after the swats we left their bedrooms until they stopped crying. Then we returned and again reviewed why they were punished.

Fifth, after we talked things over, we held them in our arms, hugged them, and told them we loved them. Then we ended the process with a word of prayer. We enjoy very special memories of these moments of shared love.

In this age of child abuse, some parents are reluctant to spank or punish their children for disobedience. But punishment following God's guidelines can be effective when administered in love. Don't punish when you are angry or emotionally out of control. Remember that the goal of punishment is to return our children to positive training.

For lesser infractions we used other forms of discipline such as restrictions and grounding. As they reached driving age, we used the car as a pawn for discipline. The privilege of having car keys was a great motivator for positive behavior.

One Saturday afternoon, Jenny, who was a young teen at the time, was shopping with friends while Emilie and I worked in the yard. The mother of one of Jenny's friends brought Jenny home later than expected. The woman explained that the group of girls had been detained by the department store's security personnel because one of the other girls was suspected of stealing some fingernail polish.

When the others had gone I was so upset that Jenny was involved that I wanted to punish her immediately. But I sensed God telling me to send her to her room to read 1 John 1:9: "If we confess our sins, He is faithful and righteous to forgive us our sins and to cleanse us from all unrighteousness" (NASB). I said, "Jenny, when you are ready to talk about this situation, come out and we will talk."

While she was in her room my emotions ranged from anger to tears of disappointment. Then an amazing thing happened to me. I caught a glimpse of how God must feel about me when I sin. I realized that God has forgiven me all my unrighteousness. If God could forgive me, I could certainly forgive my daughter for being involved with a suspected shoplifter.

Jenny must have stayed in her room for at least 30 minutes, but it seemed like three hours to me. When she finally came out she had her Bible in her hand and tears in her eyes. I gave her a big hug and told her that we loved her. We sat down together and talked and prayed about what she and the other girls had done. Together we asked God for forgiveness. I had her write the date in the margin next to 1 John 1:9. Today when she reads that verse her mind flashes back to that Saturday when she learned that God does cleanse us from all unrighteousness when we confess our sins.

When Jenny told her friend what had happened at home, she said, "You are really lucky to have a dad like you have." Jenny felt so proud of our family and she never had any problems like that again.

Each child responds differently to punishment. What is effective for one child may have no impact on the other children in the family. Our goal was to control our children's behavior in the most gentle and considerate way possible. Emilie and I always watched to see if the child was genuinely sorry for his misbehavior after punishment. We felt our punishment was effective when Jenny or Brad expressed in words or tears that they knew what they did was wrong, that they agreed that our standard was fair, and that they intended not to violate the standard again.

Know Your Child's Temperament

In an earlier chapter we recommended Dr. Tim LaHaye's book, *The Spirit-Controlled Temperament*, as an excellent resource for understanding our differences as husband and wife according to the four temperaments—sanguine, melancholy, choleric, and phlegmatic. In her book, *Your Personality Tree*, Florence Littauer gives her overview of the four temperaments so parents can better understand their children and their differences. She states: "We as parents have an obligation and duty before God to discern that way of each child and endeavor to maximize strengths and diminish weaknesses in the most loving way possible. With an understanding of temperaments we have tools readily available."[1]

Emilie and I have found that understanding the temperaments gives parents a special grasp of the needs of each child. Far too often we parents want to change our children's temperaments to meet our expectations. But after raising our own two children, and starting anew with our grandchildren, we see more clearly how important it is to discipline each child within the scope of what God wants him to be. An awareness of the four temperaments can help us do that.

The Sanguine Child

Your lively, bright-eyed sanguine child is full of curiosity and laughter. He may not always have an audience, but that never seems to stop the constant chatter which is the first step toward that center-stage personality. This child is full of wonderful creative ideas, but is often defeated in carrying them out by a short attention span which keeps him from doing as well as others academically. Education takes a backseat to more important pursuits such as cheer-leading, drama class, student council, dancing lessons, or anything else that will provide an escape from the books.

Our daughter Jenny is a good example of the sanguine personality. From kindergarten through high school she was a talker in school. She was a cheer-leader from the seventh grade through the first two years of college. When she met Craig her enthusiasm for fun followed her into their married life. She and Craig once owned an aerobic exercise studio, and she continues to teach aerobics at a health studio. Her daughter Christine is just like her.

Popularity and acceptance is an overwhelming need for this child. The sanguine child is the most likely to go along with the crowd or be drawn into an unwise situation by friends. When he tells a fib it is out of his need for approval, often gaining attention from his wild and colorful stories. Look for this child to come up with endless excuses to avoid unpleasant confrontations. A parent's disappointment or anger spells rejection for him, and he will avoid rejection at all costs. But even when the sanguine child is punished, he will soon forget the rejection and will not hold a grudge or sulk for long.

The sanguine child should be encouraged in the areas of performance: singing, dancing, acting, art, sports, etc. Because of a short attention span this child will have difficulty with activities such as piano which requires diligent practice. Find at least one activity in which your child shows skill and then encourage, encourage, encourage. He will accomplish more from one word of encouragement from you than from your yelling, criticizing, or constant spanking.

This child will only do well in a duty if it is transformed into a game with a prize as motivation. Sometimes peer approval will provide the impetus, but often a parent will need to stay alongside the child until the unpleasant task is completed successfully. This child has a greater need for physical affection than those of other temperaments, so parents need to cushion their discipline in a lot of hugging, holding, and touching.

Start early to teach this child the discipline of a clean room and the importance of handling money wisely. Understand that you will need to stay right with this child to guarantee any kind of results in training. Without such a commitment from parents this child can easily slip into irresponsibility.

The Melancholy Child

Of all the temperaments, the melancholy child is the most creative and genius-prone. Some parents actually feel threatened by the innate mental capacities of such a child. The melancholy child is deeply sensitive and has a propensity to withdraw when he really wants to reach out. In early childhood this child has a great need for physical closeness with his parents. As a result, he can be damaged by neglect or abuse during childhood more than any other personality.

These gentle, sensitive children are easily wounded and frightened. Their insecurities make them vulnerable to outside substances which offer to provide confidence or to relieve their depression. Many alcoholics, drug addicts, and homosexuals appear to be of the melancholy temperament.

The melancholy child often strives for perfection in many areas of his life. He will seldom need prodding in school, for he will be a good student with very high standards. Our son Brad displayed strong melancholy traits like perfectionism as early as age three. When we had catsup on the table for a meal, Brad always had to wipe off the top of the bottle before replacing the cap after use. During his three-year high school football career, Brad's team had an outstanding record of 33-3. But as a melancholy child, Brad had a difficult time with those three losses. He would dissect each play to see how his team could have won those games.

One of the great struggles for the melancholy child is in the area of negative thought patterns and a refusal to communicate his needs before his feelings are hurt. This inability to communicate causes him to internalize his need for approval rather than openly seek approval as the sanguine child will. He feels if you really love him you will sense his need for approval without him telling you. Teaching this child to communicate his needs and feelings will help to short-circuit his chronic moodiness and unhappiness.

Because he has such a vivid visual memory and tendency toward intense reaction, keep your melancholy child away from disturbing entertainment such as depressing literature and music, and television programs or movies filled with horror or violence. Such input is not good for any child, but the melancholy child may be seriously affected by trauma dramas.

Beginning early in his childhood, direct the melancholy mind toward the positives of life. Spend time often having him list the good things God has done for him or given him. Teach him early that our Lord allows both successes and failures into each of our lives. Explain that each setback we face makes us more compassionate toward others who are hurting.

The Choleric Child

The choleric child is the original strong-willed child, full of energy, adventure, and impatience. This child is born to lead, and expresses it early through his demands and tantrums. Control is the key word to understanding the choleric. Whether through his positive leadership or negative angry outbursts, the choleric must be in control.

The choleric child can be a very productive powerhouse, able to make quick and competent decisions and often outsmart his parents. He is full of confidence and pride, and is often bossy and tactless in his relationships. Our little grandson Chad shows choleric tendencies when he points his finger to emphasize his statements and when he wants his younger sister Christine to do things his way. When Chad is unruly, Jenny takes him aside, looks him in the eyes, and neutralizes his bossiness with a firm voice and touch.

The choleric child has the greatest potential for leadership, either positive or negative. This adventuresome child needs challenge and change. Keep him busy and give him responsibilities to help him remain productive. If he isn't in control of something such as his room, the dog, or the backyard, he will exert his need for control on his friends at school. Because they are so bossy, cholerics often have poor peer relationships.

Because of his innate logic he will thrive on educational toys, puzzles, and play times that allow for the expression of leadership. But since he craves control, he is always thinking and plotting way ahead of parents, teachers, and friends. As the parent of a choleric child, you must be loving but firm. He must know that you mean what you say in your training and punishment.

It is important to stand toe-to-toe with this strong-willed child in discipline no matter what the cost. You need to break his will without breaking his spirit. If you aren't consistent with your discipline and follow-through he will soon be in charge of you. Furthermore, be sure to reason sensibly with him, for he will tend to rebel when discipline or demands lack a logical explanation. Respect his need for fairness and justice, and be open and honest with him or he will catch you in your inconsistencies.

Since the choleric child is short on mercy and tenderness, it is important to utilize each of his struggles to teach him how to handle his hurts and disappointments and understand the struggles of others. Don't let him develop an attitude of superiority which causes him to look down on others as "dummies."

The Phlegmatic Child

The easy-going phlegmatic child, who is content with a life of eating and sleeping, is seldom a problem. He requires minimal care and attention. Phlegmatics can entertain themselves easily and it takes little to make them happy. Of all infants, they are the most calm, agreeable, and understanding. The phlegmatic child prefers to watch the world go by because watching requires less effort than getting involved. Every action is subconsciously evaluated in terms of how much energy is required, and few activities are worth the effort to him. (At times we might think that all teenagers are phlegmatics. I know we did.)

This child is not openly rebellious, but possesses a quiet will of iron. He may outwardly smile and agree to whatever you ask when he has no intention of complying. He may even lie to avoid any form of conflict or contention. He doesn't set out to be dishonest, but if shifting blame will eliminate responsibility, he's willing to take the chance.

While the phlegmatic child is a good listener and peacemaker, his indecisiveness and lack of motivation can paralyze him with procrastination and inactivity. A choleric parent cannot understand why a phlegmatic child has no ambition.

Emilie and Brad both masked being phlegmatics when they were young. Emilie had a very domineering father and she didn't want to make waves, so she became a very quiet phlegmatic-like peacemaker. After we were married she became confident in our relationship and learned to trust me. Then her true temperaments emerged—choleric and sanguine. Brad was the youngest in a very active family of sanguines and cholerics. He said, "No way am I going to tackle this group," so he masked his true temperament with passive, phlegmatic behavior. Not until he entered college and became involved in a fraternity did his natural melancholy and choleric traits fully emerge.

Since the phlegmatic is driven by his need for peace, he can become physically ill when faced with conflict. When forced to deal with another's anger, he may draw a mental blank. As such, he has a deep need to feel special to someone; so don't ignore him just because he is not demanding. Value your phlegmatic child and let him know that you do.

Seek to involve this child in physical activities such as sports, gymnastics, or dancing. He may not do well in team sports because he has little drive and he may upset his teammates when he is dreaming in left field.

The phlegmatic child has the least natural imagination of all the temperaments, so begin reading to him early and stimulate his creativity through games of make-believe and mental challenge. This is the most difficult child to direct toward a lifetime work because there is little a phlegmatic gets sufficiently excited about to make him persist to a positive conclusion. Present simple choices to him and praise him warmly for making his own decisions, even if they aren't the choices you would make.

This child is the most underdeveloped in the area of expressing anger. But since anger must find some form of expression, it often bubbles up in the phlegmatic as sarcasm. Help him understand the link between sarcasm and anger and how this type of humor can destroy friendships. Direct him to some creative outlets for his repressed anger through "talking out" his responses to conflict in a nonthreatening environment.[2]

Plant What You Want to Grow

When I go to the nursery to select my seeds for spring and summer planting, I am overwhelmed at the variety of seeds available. You can't just ask for radish seeds or squash seeds; you must ask for the particular kind of radish seeds and squash seeds you want. Recently Emilie planted seeds for a certain variety of pumpkin she thought would be nice for Halloween. We thought little of the words on the package, "These pumpkins can grow to 100 pounds each." But these pumpkin plants began to grow like Jack's bean stalk. They took over everything in the garden and produced some huge pumpkins.

The disciplining of children is like the tending of a garden. You must be careful to plant by the words you use what you really want to grow in their hearts. First you have to continually pull out the weeds of bad communication and water the seeds of positive, edifying communication. If you bad-mouth them, talk down to them, or criticize them, they will grow up to display the negative fruit of the verbal seeds you plant. But if you praise them, encourage them, honor them, and compliment them, they will grow up producing positive fruit. Mark Twain's statement will be true of them: "I can live for two months on a good compliment."

Well-chosen words will communicate your belief in your children. As a junior high student, Brad was involved in a situation in which his statement on a behavior problem conflicted with the statements of his fellow students. After listening to both sides of the story, I looked Brad in the eyes and said, "Brad, I believe you are telling the truth." My position on Brad's statement was very unpopular because the other students swore that Brad was wrong. But within a week, one of the other student's mothers called us to say her child had confessed that Brad had not been involved in the problem—just as Brad had said.

You can imagine what this experience did for Brad's relationship with his father. I believed in him, and to this day Brad shares about the positive impact my words of confidence had on his life. Your children will usually *become* what you tell them they *are*. Your words of belief in them communicate your trust, and your children will be motivated to prove themselves worthy of your trust. Galatians 6:9 states: "In due time we shall reap if we do not grow weary" (NASB). There may be days when you feel like quitting because you don't see the fruit of your labor. But continue to pray and hang in there and you will reap what you sow in your children's lives.

12

Feathering a Great Nest— Full or Empty

> She watches carefully all that goes on throughout her household, and is never lazy. Her children stand to bless her; so does her husband (Prov. 31:27-28, TLB).

When God created Eve out of Adam's rib, He equipped her with unique characteristics which complemented her husband. Apparently one of the characteristics God invested in Eve and her female descendants was the nesting instinct. Bob and I have noticed that most of the women we meet in seminars have a desire to create and maintain a warm, attractive home for themselves, their husbands, and their children. Though we express it in many different ways, we women seem to be more home-oriented than our husbands.

The changing role of women in our society has tended to submerge the nesting instinct, and today's female doesn't operate much like Grandma did. Women today don't cook, clean, iron, or mother like previous generations. Careers are more popular with women, and many are forced to work to support an affluent life-style. In many cases a couple cannot even buy a home unless both partners are working full time.

Children are often the neglected victims of the woman's misplaced nesting instinct. Child-care centers and extended day schools are almost a necessity in our society. One preschool teacher I met said the children she cares for are with her an average of 11 hours a day. Today's mothers are trusting other people to raise their children. Mom picks up her kids after a hard day's work, races through the fast-food restaurant on the way home, and then kicks off her shoes and passes out. There is no time for nesting and mothering. Older latch-key kids come home to an empty house where potato chips and television are their best friends. Whatever happened to homemade cookies and milk and warm comments like, "Tell me about your day" and "May I help you with your homework?"

Today a homemaker committed to nesting and mothering is often seen as inferior to a career-oriented woman. If she teaches someone else's children she is given the title of teacher; if she teaches her own children she is just a mother. If she chooses paint, wallpaper, and fabric for others she is an interior decorator; if she decorates her own home she's just a homemaker. If she professionally cares for the bumps and bruises of others she is a nurse; if she cares for her children's physical needs she is only a mom doing her job. Mothers employ the skills of many professions, but often receive much less recognition than professional women.

The Rewarding Joy of Nesting

I loved my role as a wife and mother, and I continually endeavored to keep our nest warm. I worked at organizing my time to care for five children so I had time for other activities. It was important to me to exchange recipes, be involved at church, and be available for Bob's needs. Caring for my family was exciting to me, but I didn't depend on them for all my strokes. Reaching out to other activities brought a balance to my life. As the children got older I taught a Bible study and built a thriving business in my home. But my activities were always subject to my priorities of seeking the Lord first, being a helpmate to Bob, guiding our children, and keeping our nest clean.

My friend Barbara is a master at making her family's nest a joyful and comfortable place. When her family goes on vacation, Barbara takes her nest with her. Upon arrival at the hotel or motel, she pulls out a checked tablecloth, candles, crackers, and cheese. She brings flowers to place by the bed and a perfumed candle or spray enhance the bathroom. When her children were small Barbara brought games, popcorn, crayons, and each child's favorite pillow, toy, or "blankie" on each trip. Barbara keeps building her nest wherever the family goes. The effort isn't great—throwing a few extra things in a suitcase or backpack. But the effort expended is sure worth the positive results.

The story of Sarah Edwards, a model mother and nest builder of the 18th century, is fascinating. Sarah was married to a famous clergyman and theologian and was the mother of 11 children. She was a deeply Christian woman, patient but firm, who treated her children with courtesy and love. She had the ability to guide her children without angry words or blows. Unlike many mothers today, Sarah Edwards had only to speak once to her children and they obeyed. They were taught proper manners and deep respect for their parents. When Mr. and Mrs. Edwards entered the room, the children rose instinctively and remained standing until their parents were seated. Being loved and well-treated by their parents, Sarah's children learned to love and respect their parents and each other.

In the management of her busy nest, Sarah Edwards put her modern-day counterparts to shame. We who have only to press a button to accomplish a domestic chore can hardly imagine the physical labor required of a colonial homemaker. In addition to caring for her 11 children, Sarah was responsible for making the candles and the clothes, growing and preparing the food, stoking the fire, and housing and feeding the numerous guests of a respected clergyman. She taught her children how to work, clearly defined the boundaries for their behavior, and tolerated no misbehavior. The result was a household which emanated love and harmony.

What were the long-term results of Sarah Edwards' investment in her family? A study of some 1,400 descendants of the Edwards family revealed the following accomplishments: 13 college presidents; 65 professors; 100 lawyers; the dean of a law school; 30 judges; 66 physicians; the dean of a medical school; 80 holders of public office; three U.S. senators; three mayors of large cities; three state governors; one vice president of the United States; and one controller of the U.S. treasury. Much of the character of these descendants was the result of the nesting endeavors of Sarah Edwards.

Sarah Edwards, like many wives and mothers today, had a full-time profession as a homemaker. We should never feel guilty because we work full time at home. Could Sarah have done her nesting job as well while maintaining a full-time profession outside the home? Hardly! Don't be discouraged if your nesting activities prevent you, at least temporarily, from another career. Someday, like Sarah Edwards, you will be able to look back and appreciate the fruit of your investment in the lives of your children and their children.

The Ministry of the Nest

Building a nest and nurturing a family takes lots of love, time, and energy. But it is a ministry which must be faithfully performed as to the Lord. For example, Jane, a mother of two preschool daughters, complained to me in tears one morning, "I'm exhausted all the time, my house is a mess, and the girls are driving me up the wall. To top it all off, my husband expects me to pack a lunch for him every day. That's too much to ask! What does he do for me? I'd pack a lunch for anyone but him."

"You would?" I asked, and Jane nodded. "Wonderful! Tonight before you go to bed, pack a lunch for the Lord and put it in the refrigerator. Set out a place mat with a bowl, some cereal, and a glass for juice or milk. Then write a note to the Lord which says, 'I love you. Your lunch is in the refrigerator,' and leave it on the table." Jane agreed to my plan.

The next time we met Jane told me that the first lunch she packed was for the Lord, and so was the second. But by the third day, as she was spreading the mustard, she realized that her service to the Lord and her service to her husband were one in the same. Her attitude began to change toward her husband and toward her role as a wife and a mother.

We met frequently after that and Jane displayed a teachable spirit and a willingness to serve God by serving her family. She began to rise early in the morning, plan her schedule and menu, set goals, turn the TV off, and tend to her nest conscientiously. Today Jane has three lovely girls and a happy husband, and she teaches our "More Hours in My Day" seminar in Illinois—all because she was willing to pack a lunch for the Lord.

Gina's story is a sad illustration of what can happen when we neglect the Lord and our nests. At one time Gina and her husband and three children were a committed church family, and Gina was a contributing member of a Bible study group I led. Gina's home was a warm and happy nest where her children were taught Christian songs and were involved in healthy activities.

I first noticed Gina's problem when she dropped out of our Bible study group. She went to work, had a hysterectomy, received a breast implant, and lost her extra weight. She attended her high school reunion and within a year her warm, loving nest was blown apart. She rekindled her love for her high school sweetheart, left her husband and children, and went out into the world to "find herself."

The basic reason for unhappy homes like Gina's is a departure from God's Word about what a warm, loving nest should be. Gina's trouble began when she neglected her relationship with God and subsequently rejected His plan for her role in the family. The result of disobedience is anguish and suffering for every member of the family, especially the children.

But even broken lives can be rebuilt when commitment to Christ and His Word are honored. After her second divorce, Georgia committed her love and her life to Christ. Her previous two non-Christian marriages had fallen apart, so she wasn't about to make the same mistake again. But Georgia was a beautiful woman and had no problem attracting available men. Georgia met Jim, a successful businessman with all the qualities Georgia had dreamed of in a husband,

and they fell in love. But Jim was divorced, an alcoholic, and an unbeliever. Georgia was ready to leap from the frying pan into the fire.

One night after our aerobic class I challenged Georgia to stand on her love and commitment to Christ. I urged her to trust Christ for her future and not to become unequally yoked with an unbeliever. "Tell Jim that Christ is the number one priority in your life," I counseled. "Insist that if Jim is to come into the picture and build a nest with you, it must be with Christ at the center of both of your lives." Before we left the dressing room that night Georgia and I prayed together about the situation.

Later that night Georgia met Jim and told him of her love for Jesus. She led him to the Lord and convinced him to join Alcoholics Anonymous. With Christ at the center of their relationship, Georgia and Jim began their recovery from the broken nests of the past. They were married in our home on our 28th wedding anniversary, so we share the same wedding date. Today they are still experiencing a growing, loving relationship with the Lord and with each other. They are living proof that God can restore, remodel, rebuild, and refurbish our broken, torn, and fragmented nests.

When the Chicks Leave the Nest

I remember saying to myself when our children were young, "I can't wait until Brad and Jenny grow up and go to college. Then I can have time for me. I can sleep as late as I want. The house will be clean and uncluttered all the time. Peanut butter and honey will be in the cupboard instead of on the kitchen floor. I can set a table for two every night with quiet music and candlelight for just Bob and me. No more baby-sitters to schedule, skinned knees to worry about, chicken pox, homework, bikes, or roller skates. It will be wonderful!"

The excitement mounted the day I helped Jenny load her V.W. convertible as she prepared to leave for college. Finally she started the engine and drove away from the curb. I stood in the middle of our residential street waving good-bye until she was out of sight. This was the day I had been waiting for. Our two little monkeys were gone at last. I was so happy!

As I walked back into the house and up the stairs I prayed for Jenny and her college days ahead. I went into Jenny's room and found everything neat and in order. Her bed was perfectly made with the pillows placed just right. From there I went into Brad's room. Brad had been gone for two years, but his room was still decorated with trophies, yearbooks, photos, and a big trash basket stuffed with a basketball, volleyball, football, and tennis balls. Brad's bed was made without one lump. Yes, the children were finally gone and everything was perfect.

As I walked down the hall toward our bedroom it hit me: I was 38 years old and I was no longer a mom. My children didn't need me anymore. Bob was striving to become a mobile home tycoon and he didn't really need me. And I was so organized by 8:10 every morning as a homemaker that my house didn't need me either. I had lost my identity. "Emilie, who are you?" I wondered frantically. I threw myself on the bedroom floor and began to cry out to God. "Who am I? What happens next? Who cares about me?"

I remained on the floor for a long time until some words from the Psalms came into my heart and found their way to my lips. Speaking to the Lord, David wrote: "You chart the path ahead of me, and tell me where to stop and rest. Every moment you know where I am.... You saw me before I was born and scheduled each day of my life before I began to breathe. Every day was recorded in your Book!" (Ps. 139:3,16, TLB). I thought surely this day could not have been scheduled by God. Children leaving the nest was supposed to bring happiness and rest. But instead I was suddenly in the midst of mid-life crisis.

I reached for my Bible, turned to Psalm 139, and read it repeatedly. Soon David's prayer in verse 23 became my prayer: "Search me, O God, and know my heart; test my thoughts. Point out anything you find in me that makes you sad, and lead me along the path of everlasting life" (TLB). That day on the floor I committed myself—as a woman in an empty nest—completely to God. "I'm yours, Lord," I prayed. "Mold me and guide me to be the woman you want me to be. Use any talents and gifts you have given me to glorify Your name."

Perhaps you are facing the same disturbing questions today which I cried out to God the day Jenny left home. You're lonely, tired, and have no direction for your life beyond the empty nest. I encourage you to saturate your heart with Psalm 139, especially the prayer in verse 23. Ask God to forgive your past and submit yourself, your talents, and your gifts to Him. Submit to God's direction in prayer daily and thank Him for what He is going to do in your life beyond the empty nest.

Opportunities Outside the Nest

On the day of my commitment on the bedroom floor God began to set in motion a new ministry for Bob and me. I began teaching a few women's seminars on home organization and time management. During this time I met Florence Littauer, who has become a friend and a mentor. She encouraged me to put my material into a book and introduced me to Harvest House which published my first book, *More Hours in My Day*. Since then six more books have been published, and God has given Bob and me the opportunity to speak to hundreds of couples in our seminar ministry. It has all come about because I committed myself to God in the midst of a mid-life crisis.

Your years of active parenting occupy only about a third of your adult life, so you have lots of time to develop other interests and dabble in other activities. Perhaps you'd like more schooling. Great! Take some classes or get the degree you missed out on during the nesting years. Take some special interest classes and cultivate the desires of your heart. My friend Donna loves to cook Chinese food, and has taught several of us how to make won ton soup and Chinese chicken salad. She discovered her unique cooking talent after her children were gone.

I've always been interested in nutrition, so I began reading and talking with informed women on the subject. Sue Gregg came into my life, and together we wrote *Eating Right* (Harvest House). This all took place ten years after Jenny left home for college.

If you especially love children, become a nanny or start a child-care service in your home or church. You may want to get involved in teaching child evangelism classes in your neighborhood like my friend Colleen does. Today's children desperately need the Christian love and influence of someone with a quiet and gentle spirit.

The empty nest years are an opportunity to develop yourself physically. You may want to jog or do aerobic exercises. Physical activity will give you energy and new interest. I walk two miles every day. I use this time to praise God and pray. Six other women also walk my route and they exchange recipes, books, and ideas. Exercise is a way to meet new people and expand your mind while cultivating a healthy body.

Think about starting a new career or launching a business in your home. Gary and Carolyn started a woodworking business which has grown to become "The Country Carpenter." Gary cuts the wood patterns and Carolyn hand paints them. They sell their products all over the United States. Kim loves to cook, so she prepares casseroles from our *Eating Right* cookbook and sells them out of her freezer. She's doing very well at it.

Debra took my idea for the "love basket" and added her personal touch by creating baskets for all occasions. She puts items in each basket which fit the occasion—anniversary, baby shower, get well, holidays, "I love you," etc. She sells her baskets to businessmen in office buildings, secretaries, friends, and others. Other women I know have operated full or part-time businesses in their homes with national companies like Amway, Shaklee, Mary Kay, Home Interiors, Princess House crystal, and Tupperware. Use your creative resources and put yourself to work with the talents God has given you.

Become a Titus 2 Woman

The apostle Paul wrote: "Older women must train the younger women to live quietly, to love their husbands and their children, and to be sensible and clean minded, spending their time in their own homes, being kind and obedient to their husbands, so that the Christian faith can't be spoken against by those who know them" (Titus 2:4-5, TLB). As a young wife and mother, my heart's desire was to be the kind of younger woman Paul described in these verses. I was a new

Christian and I knew I needed the influence and teaching of older women. But when I was invited to a women's prayer group I didn't want to go. I was afraid to pray out loud and the thought of a being with praying women intimidated me. Yet something inside me kept saying, "Go, go, go." So with much resistance from my flesh I attended my first prayer group meeting.

The atmosphere in Jan King's home was so cozy and the other women were so warm and friendly. I was impressed by the presence of the Spirit there. And Jan had real china cups and saucers! She poured coffee and tea for us and fresh flowers adorned the table. I was impressed with these women, many of whom were much older than I. They were real women with heart. The prayer time was very simple. They prayed just like they talked, sometimes even laughing in their prayers.

I cried all the way home that morning. My heart was so filled with God's love poured through the women who accepted me and prayed for me. They were the older women described in Titus 2 that I so desperately needed in my life. I couldn't wait for the next prayer group meeting. Over the years these Titus 2 women have taught me much. I learned from them how to pray and serve coffee in china cups. What beautiful models they have been to me. Many of them are still my special friends more than 25 years later.

As your children grow up and your nesting responsibilities diminish, you have the opportunity to share what you have learned with younger women (and men). You may want to host a Bible study and prayer group for young women or couples. I remember the evening Bob and I started a college Bible study group in our home. No one showed up that first Thursday evening, but after two years we had over 60 students attending regularly.

When Brad's best friend Todd was killed at age 16, we started a neighborhood women's Bible study for his mother to help love her through her grief. Three women came the first morning, but the group lasted 14 years. Many women's lives were touched and changed, and many marriages were strengthened and reconciled through that group. It all began because I determined to follow through with the modeling of the Titus 2 women who had touched my life.

We need more Titus 2 women in our churches and neighborhoods today. As your nest empties, you have more time to devote to being a loving, teaching model of Christian womanhood. You can sit back and watch forever. How much better to reach out and teach those things you have learned in your nesting years to those who need to learn them now.

Spiritual sisters are a great help at this time in your life—others you can trust, love, hug, pray with, and cry with. Women need women to talk with and pray with. God created us so uniquely complex, filled with qualities which need to be expressed and shared. So swallow your fears and run with the Lord. Prepare yourself to be used of God as a mentor to other women.

Growing in Grandparenting

Bob and I have not had a perfect marriage, nor have we grown perfect children. But God gave us a second chance at parenting when our Jenny married Craig and in time they presented us with three adorable grandchildren. A second chance? You bet! We have opportunities with our grandchildren that we never took with our children. We realize the importance of time and priorities. Parents of young children are caught up in the overwhelming task of making a living, providing shelter, food, clothing, vacations, schooling, and everything else they think they need to keep up with today's life-style. As grandparents, we have won most of those battles and have the time, energy, and resources to spend with our three grandchildren that we didn't have with Jenny and Brad.

When our children were young my priorities for nesting and parenting were a little out of balance. I thought the kitchen floor needed to be mopped and shined every day. Sometimes cleaning that kitchen floor was more important to me than spending time with my children. But in 33-plus years of marriage we've had nine different kitchen floors, and none of them was as important as Jenny and Brad. Now, when our grandchildren come over, the kitchen floor is where Bob and I often sit and play blocks, cars, paper dolls, and games with them. To us as grandparents, a floor is not something to mop, it's another tool by which we creatively build great grandchildren. Time spent growing great grandchildren is more important than time spent mopping floors.

To Chad, Bevan, and Christine, Bob is Papa Bob and I am Grammie Em. Bob is a great Papa. He takes the kids on walks, out to lunch, to the pet store, and to the animal park and Kiddyland. He digs holes in the backyard with the boys and teaches them how to plant, grow, and water a garden (and how they love to water!). Bob even built a tree house for the children in our yard, complete with slide, swings, and a fireman's pole and rope climb. Our grandchildren love their Papa because he is their friend, always ready to share a smile, crack a joke, and give them "butterfly kisses." As they grow they will find fishing, hiking, and ball-playing to be a major part of Papa's involvement with them.

We have a great time dramatizing the Wizard of Oz with the children. Papa is the lion and he hides in the bushes. Chad is the scarecrow, Bevan is Toto the dog, Christine is Dorothy, and I am the wicked witch of the north. We skip down the yellow brick road looking for the Wizard of Oz. Anyone who happens to be watching would think we were crazy—two 50-year-olds (plus) acting so silly. But we don't care because our little ones are so ecstatic that we all participate.

When Christine was two-and-a-half years old we had our first tea party. We laid a tablecloth on the floor and used real cups, saucers, and cloth napkins. I served cinnamon tea and oatmeal cookies, and Christine picked a few flowers for the occasion. We even lit a candle. We pretended to be mommies and talked about grown-up things. Raggedy Ann and Teddy joined us. We continue to have tea parties and even invite Papa and the boys sometimes. What a teaching tool tea parties are for helping our grandchildren learn about contributing to a great nest. They have all learned how to mix cookie dough, bake bread, fix pancakes, and wash dishes with joy.

We have discovered many creative ways of keeping the grandchildren busy. I have a box full of old dress-up clothes such as high heels, costume jewelry, gloves, hats, and purses. What fun our grandchildren have dressing themselves up. And Papa and Grammie often join in the fun. We've acted out weddings with Papa as the pastor, complete with a real Bible and real flowers. Boxes of dress-up clothes make great gifts for grandchildren.

One day we were baby-sitting the grandchildren and came up with the cutest idea. Bob unrolled some brown wrapping paper on the kitchen floor (there's that great floor again!). We laid each child on the paper in order to trace the outline of their bodies.

Then we cut out each body outline and the grandchildren had a great time decorating themselves on paper. They used old yarn for hair, colored in the clothes with crayons, and even glued buttons on the clothes. How excited they were to take their paper people home.

We have also been blessed with the opportunity to teach our grandchildren about the Lord by acting out Bible stories with them, reading the Bible to them, and praying with them. Recently Chad asked me to pray for a friend at his preschool who needs to love Jesus. And when I ask Christine how I can pray for her, she is beginning to give me her requests.

You may say that all this active grandparenting takes a lot of time. You bet! But somehow we include it in between teaching seminars, writing books, and traveling. We have found that we will do whatever we really want to do. And Bob and I really want to be a godly Papa and Grammie and help grow great grandchildren. Who else would allow children to smear soap, lipstick, and rouge all over their faces? Only a committed Grammie and Papa.

We are blessed that our grandchildren live nearby. But grandparents whose grandchildren are cities, states, or countries away can still grandparent. Send the grandchildren cards, letters, and gifts often. They'll love photos of Grandpa and Grandma and their cat, dog, bird, or house—anything to identify you with them. Send them an audio or video tape of you reading a story, praying for them, or singing or playing an instrument for them. They will enjoy playing the tape over and over.

If you don't have any grandchildren of your own, borrow some. "Adopt" the children of a young couple in your church or neighborhood who have no living grandparents or whose grandparents live far away.

Invest your empty nest time and resources in some little lives you can help shape.

Grandparenting doesn't end when the grandchildren reach the teenage years or adulthood. As long as we grandparents are alive we have the opportunity to impact our grandchildren. I talk with many grandparents who hurt for their teenage or adult grandchildren in their complicated, trouble-filled lives. We may think that our role is over once they begin their own homes and families. But life is really just beginning for them, and they need our support and encouragement more than ever.

One of our primary commitments to our grandchildren is to pray for them. We pray for their spiritual development, trusting God that one day they will all desire to serve Him. Trials, troubles, and grief have hit our family several times during our marriage. And as our family grows in number, our trials also seem to grow. But our prayers for our children and grandchildren are based on the promise of Psalm 73:26: "My mind and my body may grow weak, but God is my strength. He is all I ever need" (TEV). If we could only remember that seven days without prayer makes one *weak*. The key to growing great grandchildren is growing grandparents who pray for them.

Whenever we say good-bye to the grandchildren in person or over the phone, there are two things we always say: "I love you" and "God bless you." Now that they are growing older, guess what we hear back from them: "I love you, Grammie and Papa. God bless you." Who says there are no rewards for being grandparents!

"More Hours in My Day" can provide many of the organizational materials that are recommended in this book and others written by Emilie Barnes. You may obtain a price list and seminar information by sending your request and a stamped, self-addressed business envelope to:

More Hours in My Day
2838 Rumsey Drive
Riverside, CA 92506

Notes

Chapter 4—Great Marriages Need Great Wives

1. Dennis and Barbara Rainey, *Building Your Mate's Self-Esteem* (Here's Life Publishers, 1986), p. 35.
2. Linda Dillow, *Creative Counterpart* (Thomas Nelson, Inc., 1977), p. 54.
3. Ibid., p. 109.

Chapter 5—Great Marriages Need Great Husbands

1. Rainey, op. cit., p. 35.
2. Jay Adams, *Christian Living in the Home* (Baker Book House, 1972), pp. 91-92.

Chapter 6—Growing Together Despite Differences

1. Joyce Brothers, Ph.D., *What Every Woman Should Know about Men* (Ballantine Books, 1981), p. 31.
2. Doreen Kimura, "Male Brain, Female Brain: The Hidden Difference," *Psychology Today*, November, 1985, p. 56.
3. William and Nancy Carmichael with Dr. Timothy Boyd, *That Man! Understanding the Difference between You and Your Husband* (Thomas Nelson Publishers, 1988), adapted from chapter 2.
4. Warren Farrell, *Why Men Are the Way They Are* (McGraw Hill Book Company, 1986), adapted from p. 139.
5. Carol Gilligan, *In a Different World* (Harvard University Press, 1981), p. 8.
6. Carmichael, op. cit., adapted from chapter 4.
7. You may contact Florence Littauer's office regarding books, tapes, teaching materials, and information on C.L.A.S.S. by writing C.L.A.S.S., 1814-E Commercenter West, San Bernardino, CA 92408.

Chapter 7—You Can't Grow if You Don't Communicate

1. Dwight Small, *After You've Said I Do* (Fleming H. Revell, 1968), p. 244.

2. H. Norman Wright, *Communication: Key to Your Marriage* (Regal Books, 1974), p. 52.
3. John Powell, *Why Am I Afraid to Tell You Who I Am?* (Argus Communications), adapted from pp. 54-62.
4. Florence Littauer, *After Every Wedding Comes a Marriage* (Harvest House, 1981), adapted from pp. 168-176.
5. Wright, op. cit., adapted from pp. 71-77.

Chapter 8—Growing into Great Sex

1. Denis Waitley, *Seeds of Greatness* (Pocket Books, Division of Simon and Schuster, Inc., 1983), p. 160.
2. David and Carole Hocking, *Bedroom Talk* (Taken from *Good Marriages Take Time*, Harvest House Publishers, 1984), p. 19.
3. Gene Getz, *The Measure of a Marriage* (Regal Books, 1980), adapted from pp. 88-92.
4. Ibid., p. 114.

Chapter 9—Money Matters in a Great Marriage

1. We are indebted to Charles O. White, a Christian attorney and tax practitioner, for sharing his insight on the topics of giving, receiving, and spending. Mr. White has conducted "Personal and Family Financial Success" seminars for more than 10 years.

Chapter 10—Growing as Great Parents

1. Ross Campbell, *How to Really Love Your Child* (Victor Books, 1983), p. 23.
2. For more information about our family conference, see Emilie's book, *Survival for Busy Women* (Harvest House Publishers, 1986), pp. 195-198.
3. Campbell, op. cit., p. 37.
4. Campbell, op. cit., pp. 32-33.

Chapter 11—Shaping Great Children through Discipline

1. Florence Littauer, *Your Personality Tree* (Word Books, 1986), p. 158.
2. Ibid., adapted from pp. 160-172.

Other Good Harvest House Reading

AFTER EVERY WEDDING COMES A MARRIAGE
by *Florence Littauer*

Learn how to maintain marital harmony through the trials of marriage. Florence discusses the complexities of marriage and suggests ways to overcome difficulties that can threaten a relationship.

GOOD MARRIAGES TAKE TIME
by *David and Carole Hocking*

Filled with teachings rooted in God's Word, this sensitive book offers help in four areas of married life: communication, sex, friends, and finances. Questions throughout the book for both husbands and wives to answer.

MARRIAGE PERSONALITIES
by *David Field*

Take a fresh look at marriage and its seven distinct personalities. Valuable information about marriage, new insights into your spouse's behavior, and an increased ability to give and receive deeper dimensions of love and joy.

FOREVER MY LOVE
by *Margaret Hardisty*

Margaret Hardisty explains what a woman wants and needs from her man, and how very much she is willing and eager to give in return. An inspirational bestseller, there are over 325,000 copies of *Forever My Love* in print.

DATING YOUR MATE
by *Rick Bundschuh* and *Dave Gilbert*

If you've ever longed to return to those wonderful, fun-filled days of "courting," then *Dating Your Mate* is for you and your spouse. Chock-full of clever ideas that will put the romance, excitement, and spontaneity back in your life, *Dating Your Mate* is a practical guide to creative fun for marrieds and yet-to-be-marrieds. Delightfully illustrated by the authors.

ROMANCE REKINDLED
by *Rick Bundschuh* and *Dave Gilbert*

A book that is sure to reignite the embers of married romance. A virtual gold mine of practical ideas that will help you: get an unromantic spouse interested, write a great love letter, create that perfect mood; and dates that will keep your romance alive throughout the years. An exciting sequel to the bestselling book *Dating Your Mate*.

Dear Reader:

We would appreciate hearing from you regarding this Harvest House nonfiction book. It will enable us to continue to give you the best in Christian publishing.

1. What most influenced you to purchase *Growing a Great Marriage*?
   ☐ Author   ☐ Recommendations
   ☐ Subject matter   ☐ Cover/Title
   ☐ Backcover copy   ☐ _____

2. Where did you purchase this book?
   ☐ Christian bookstore   ☐ Grocery store
   ☐ General bookstore   ☐ Other
   ☐ Department store

3. Your overall rating of this book:
   ☐ Excellent ☐ Very good ☐ Good ☐ Fair ☐ Poor

4. How likely would you be to purchase other books by this author?
   ☐ Very likely   ☐ Not very likely
   ☐ Somewhat likely   ☐ Not at all

5. What types of books most interest you?
   (check all that apply)
   ☐ Women's Books   ☐ Fiction
   ☐ Marriage Books   ☐ Biographies
   ☐ Current Issues   ☐ Children's Books
   ☐ Self Help/Psychology   ☐ Youth Books
   ☐ Bible Studies   ☐ Other _____

6. Please check the box next to your age group.
   ☐ Under 18   ☐ 25-34   ☐ 45-54
   ☐ 18-24   ☐ 35-44   ☐ Over 54

Mail to: Editorial Director
Harvest House Publishers
1075 Arrowsmith
Eugene, OR 97402

Name _____

Address _____

City _____ State _____ Zip _____

Thank you for helping us to help you in future publications!